TEENS TOGETHER GRIEF SUPPORT GROUP CURRICULUM: ADOLESCENCE EDITION

TEENS TOGETHER GRIEF SUPPORT GROUP CURRICULUM:

Adolescence Edition

Grades 7–12

Linda Lehmann, M.A., L. P.
Shane R. Jimerson, Ph.D.
Ann Gaasch, M.A.

Routledge
Taylor & Francis Group
New York   London

Routledge is an imprint of the
Taylor & Francis Group, an informa business

Published in 2001 by
Routledge
Taylor & Francis Group
270 Madison Avenue
New York, NY 10016

Published in Great Britain by
Routledge
Taylor & Francis Group
2 Park Square
Milton Park, Abingdon
Oxon OX14 4RN

International Standard Book Number-10: 1-58391-302-5 (Softcover)
International Standard Book Number-13: 978-1-58391-302-4 (Softcover)
Library of Congress Card Number 00-045434
Cover design by Rob Williams

Library of Congress Cataloging-in-Publication Data

Lehmann, Linda.
   Teens together grief support group curriculum : adolescence edition : grades 7-12 / Linda Lehmann, Shane R. Jimerson, Ann Gaasch.
   p. cm.
   Includes bibliographical references and index.
   ISBN 1-58391-302-5 (pbk. : alk paper)
     1. Grief in adolescence—Study and teaching. 2. Grief in adolescence—Study and teaching. 3. Teenagers and death—Study and teaching. 4. Loss (Psychology) in adolescence—Study and teaching. 5. Teenagers—Counceling of—Study and teaching.
I. Jimerson, Shane R. II. Gaasch, Ann. III. Title.
  BF724.3.G73 L44   2000
  155.9'37' 0835—dc21   00-045434

Taylor & Francis Group is the Academic Division of Informa plc.

Visit the Taylor & Francis Web site at
http://www.taylorandfrancis.com

and the Routledge Web site at
http://www.routledge-ny.com

Contents

Preface

The Teens Together grief support curriculum is intended for use with adolescence who have experienced the death of someone special to them. It was designed for use by professionals who work in schools, hospitals, hospices, mental health agencies, or any setting that serves bereaved adolescents. The curriculum contains lesson plans for 10 sessions that include age-appropriate activities that enable adolescents to approach highly sensitive and painful topics through a variety of fun and engaging activities. The user is guided through the curriculum with detailed instructions and learning objectives for each session.

The curriculum is divided by age level so that the group activities are developmentally appropriate. This design also affords the participants an opportunity to meet peers that have had a similar loss. The activities have been designed to help youth approach their grief through a variety of engaging activities that allow for the expression of their grief. The variety of activities that include drawing, sculpting, music, games, journaling, problem-solving, drama, stories, and movement, which are used throughout the curriculum to give youths an opportunity to express their grief. Participants are taught various tools that will help them cope with their grief even after the group ends. The Tasks of Grief form the path toward their healing and offer practical steps for them to take. The curriculum also provides structure participating youths can count on every session: the topics of the sessions change, the activities vary, but the format remains the same. The group sessions are intended to present youths with topics that alternate between "head work" and "heart work." Sessions that employ activities that tap into "head work" are intended to teach group members death education, coping, and self-care techniques. Sessions that tap into "heart work" are designed to help the youth get in touch with their feelings and the pain of their loss. The intent is to help them to learn about death and to explore their grief in order to understand both. It is recognized that there is no single appropriate grief sequence or experience; rather, the aim of this grief support group curriculum is to facilitate healthy variations of mourning and positive adaptations following the death of a close or special person.

Introduction

▣ Grief is a Family Process

Teens grieve within the context of the family. Loss impacts the entire family system. As part of this system, teens learn about grief through observing, listening, and talking to their family members following an early loss. Ideally, a caregiver within the teen's family will participate in an adult support group. Often groups are organized such that the caregivers attend a separate group during the same time that the teens are participating in a group. The participation of the adults is important for several reasons.

First, it is likely that the adults will be experiencing their own grief responses, and participation in the group will facilitate healthy coping. Second, through participation in the support group, these caregivers will learn about individual differences in grief reactions; in other words, even within a family, individuals can have varied grief responses. Third, these adults will better understand information communicated in the teen's groups and be more prepared to provide support for their teens.

For instance, it is important that teens understand that it is okay to be sad, mad, happy, and scared, and that it is okay to talk about these feelings. If the family does not talk about the death, share feelings, or grieve in a healthy way, it is not likely that children will. Furthermore, grief does not simply go away after a specific amount of time; it is normal for feelings to emerge years after the loss. Thus, it is important that caregivers who will be with the teen years after the support group ends are informed about the way teens mourn.

For these reasons we encourage those coordinating grief support groups for teens to also orchestrate grief support groups for adults. These curricula are designed to address key components of grief in an age-appropriate manner in an effort to facilitate healthy mourning.

▓ A Note to Group Facilitators

The grief support group curriculum is designed to provide support, not therapy. Some teens may need to receive individual or family counseling instead of or in addition to the bereavement group. While there are a range of grief responses teens may experience, it is important to note teens experiencing strong responses (either in intensity or duration) and to refer these teens for additional services. Support group facilitators are encouraged to attend to behaviors or communications that often indicate the need for referral for individual therapeutic intervention, including: if a teen gives the slightest hint of being at risk for suicide; if a teen experiences sustained denial and refuses to acknowledge the death; if the teen reports many headaches, stomachaches, and etc. (e.g., psychosomatic problems); if the teen is experiencing persistent sleep disorders such as nightmares, bed-wetting, etc.; if a teen experiences persistent guilt regarding the death; if there is a prolonged period during which a teen is unable to focus and concentrate on schoolwork, or daydreams frequently, and is unable to complete assignments; if there are severe changes in eating patterns—binge eating, not eating, etc.; if the teen acts like the deceased person in order to bring them back or to gain favor with surviving family members; if the teen displays prolonged regression to an earlier developmental level; and/or if the teen fears the illness or experiences the symptoms of the deceased. The basic idea is to be sensitive to possible maladaptive manifestations of natural grief reactions and to provide appropriate referrals to meet the needs of each teen. Any of the common grief reactions may be unhealthy if they persist or if the teen becomes consumed with a particular response. Thus, it is important to attend to both the intensity and duration of individual grief responses.

Please note that each item listed in the Materials Section of each week's curriculum is described fully in Appendix 1.

◼ INTERVIEW SAMPLE
Basic Information

Instructions for Interviewer

Introduce self and explain position in agency. Ask if now would be a good time to talk or if it would be better to set up a different time. Explain that some information is needed to register the children for the group. Complete this form. Then fill out the full interview form, one for each child.

Name of primary caregiver: _____

Address: _____

Phone number: (Home) _____ (Work) _____

(Other) _____ Okay to leave a message? Yes _____ No _____

Names of teens	Gender	Birthdate	Grade
_____	_____	_____	_____
_____	_____	_____	_____
_____	_____	_____	_____
_____	_____	_____	_____

How were you referred to our program?

_____

Name of deceased _____ Relationship _____

Cause of death _____ Date of death _____

▩ Full Interview Sample

Instructions for Interviewer

Fill out one form for each teen to be enrolled in the program. Explain to callers that they do not need to answer these questions if they don't feel comfortable, but it is very helpful if something can be learned about the teen before he or she starts the group. Explain that this information is confidential and will be shared only with the group facilitators. However, if physical or sexual abuse of a teen is reported or if it is thought that they are going to hurt themselves or someone else confidentiality will be broken and the appropriate agency will be notified. Ask if they have any questions.

Child's name: _____

Interview date: _____   Group: _____

School

Has your child ever been in a group before (include sports activities, daycare, clubs)? Describe.

_____   _____

_____   _____

Reaction to Loss

Can you tell me a little bit more about your child's relationship with the deceased?

_____   _____

_____   _____

What feelings have you observed in your child since the death (sadness, anger, fear, happiness)? How do you know what your child is feeling (by behavior, by what they say)? What feelings do you think your child might not be expressing?

_____   _____

_____   _____

_____   _____

_____   _____

What are your concerns about your child? Why are you looking for a group now?

_____

_____

_____

_____

Relationships

Do you identify with any specific religious affiliation? How was the death explained in terms of religious affiliation?

> *Note*: if interviewees are strongly religious, inform them of the group's philosophy concerning spirituality and religion.

_____

_____

_____

Health

Do you have any concerns about:

Physical Abuse _____

Sexual Abuse _____

Has your child ever:

been treated for depression _____

had thoughts about or tried to hurt him- or herself _____

had thoughts about or tried to hurt others _____

Is your child seeing a counselor? Who? Would you sign a release in case the group leaders should need or want to contact the counselor?

_____

_____

_____

Grief Support Group Curriculum

Week 1: Information Interviews

Materials

Childhood Depression Inventory (CDI)
Common Grief Reactions Checklist (CGRC)
Grief Support Groups General Information Sheet (GIS)
Pencils
(See below and Appendix 2 for for the CDI, CGRC, and GIS. See also, sample GIS
below)

Teens need a transition into the group experience. For this reason, the first session is
an information interview. Facilitators meet with the teens and their caregivers (parents
or guardians) for a 20-minute interview. This appointment allows the families to find
their way to the location of the groups, meet their facilitators, see the space in which
their groups will meet, and talk to the facilitators about the program. Having the information interview prior to their entering the group helps to lessen their fears about the
group experience, and get many of their questions about the group answered. The
session also allows the group facilitators to meet the teens and spend a little time getting to know them one-on-one.

It is important for the facilitators to gather information about the teen's developmental history and grief experiences; therefore the GIS should be asked in a
semistructured interview format with caregivers and the teen present. A GIS should be
filled out for each teen. An additional copy of the GIS, for photocopies, is included in
Appendix 2.

In this session, facilitators should gather additional pregroup participation information, including the CDI and the CGRC, which will be collected again at the end of
the 10 sessions. Information about how to obtain the CDI can be found in Appendix 1.
The CGRC is included in Appendix 2. After this initial session, the teen is then ready to
begin the group.

Grief Support Groups General Information Sheet (GIS)

Child's name: _____

Today's date: _____ Date that the loss occurred: _____

First time participant in group? Yes _____ No _____

If no, how many times has your child participated in a group

prior to the current group? _____

Who died?

Mother _____ Father _____ Sibling _____ Friend _____

Relative (specify) _____ Other (specify) _____

How close was the child to the person that died?

Not at all close _____ Somewhat close _____ Close _____ Pretty close _____

Very close _____

What was the cause of the death?

Illness _____ Accident _____ Sudden death (e.g., heart attack) _____

Suicide _____ Homicide ___

Did the child witness the death?

Yes _____ No _____

With whom does the child currently live?

Parent _____ (specify) Mother _____ Father _____ Sibling _____

Friend _____ Relative (specify) _____ Other (specify) _____

Who provides the child's primary emotional support? (All that apply)

Parent _____ Sibling _____ Friend _____ Relative (specify) _____

Mental health practitioner (specify) _____

Religious representative (e.g., nun, pastor, rabbi, priest) _____

Other (specify) _____

What other losses has the child experienced in his or her lifetime? (All that apply)

Death of a parent (specify) _____ Date of loss _____

Death of sibling (specify age of sibling) _____ Date of loss _____

Death of friend (specify) _____ Date of loss _____

Death of relative (specify) _____ Date of loss _____

Death of other significant person (specify) _____ Date of loss _____

Loss of home (specify) _____ Date of loss _____

Separation from sibling(s) (specify) _____ Date of loss _____

Loss of biological family unit: Foster care _____ or Adoption _____

Date of loss _____

Had the child experienced any of the following prior to the loss? (All that apply)

Physical abuse _____ When _____Relationship to perpetrator _____

Sexual abuse _____ When _____ Relationship to perpetrator _____

Depression _____ When _____

Suicide attempt (s) _____ When _____

Addiction/substance abuse _____ When _____

School

Does your child receive any special assistance at school such as tutoring, advanced placement, or special classes? (specify)

_____

_____

_____

Has the school environment been supportive of your child or have there been problems since the death? (provide details)

_____

_____

_____

Reaction to Loss

How does your child most easily express him- or herself (talking, writing, art, physical games)?

_____

_____

_____

What would you like the group facilitator to know about your child?

_____

_____

_____

Relationships

How would you describe your relationship with your child? How does your child relate to other family members?

_____

_____

_____

How would you describe your child's relationship with peers (ages of peers, extrovert, introvert, leader, follower)?

_____

_____

_____

Health

Does your child have any health concerns? Any allergies? Has he or she had any serious injuries or illnesses? Is your child taking any medications?

_____

What is your child's most frequent health problem?

_____

Will you give permission for a group picture to be taken?

Yes _____ No _____

Week 2: Telling My Story

The first session with the group lays the groundwork for the following sessions. The primary goal of this session is to help the teens feel comfortable with the group, by getting to know each other and the facilitators. Make a special effort to connect with every teen, as each teen's relationship with the group leader(s) is of primary importance. During this first session, the teens are presented with many new concepts. They will be introduced to the series theme, the use of check-in, and the parameters of how the group runs. They will talk about confidentiality and develop the rules for the group, so that each teen can feel safe and comfortable in expressing him- or herself. The grief keys will be introduced, as each grief key will be the focus of one or more sessions to follow. The grief keys are the things that teens can do to help them grieve in a healthy way. The facilitator will be doing a lot of talking this first session, however the teens are given an opportunity to tell their stories to each other. This is especially important, as the group gets to hear each teen's version and understanding of his or her story which will help the facilitator to help the teens and the caregivers grapple with misunderstandings or missing pieces in their stories.

Objectives

To introduce group members to each other
To define the word "grief"
To share the circumstances of the death with peer group members

Materials

Affirmations	Handout: Grief Keys
Affirmation jar	Koosh® ball
Candle	Markers
Check-in sheets	Matches
Crayons	Name tags
Drawing sheets:	Pencils
This is What I Remember about the Funeral and	Puzzle pieces
This is What I Remember about the Day	Resource list
my Special Person Died	Story cards
Folders	Tagboard

Procedures

Note: There are main activities and supplementary activities for this age level. Main activities are considered central to the topic and are given priority. Supplemental activities are done only as time permits. A star (*) by an activity denotes that this is a main activity. Unstarred activities are supplemental activities.

*Opening Activity**

Materials
    Crayons
    Games
    Name tags

As each teen arrives, write his or her name on a name tag and attach it to him or her. The facilitator also should be wearing a name tag. Be certain to spell each teen's name correctly and use the name he or she prefers. Sometimes, it is fun to allow them to draw or color on their name tags after their names have been written on them. These name tags are worn only for the first few weeks. Because the groups are limited in size, the teens and facilitators usually learn each other's name after the first couple of weeks. Provide a few games for those who arrive early.

When everyone arrives, explain, "Each week we are going to start and end our group the same way, with a song." Teens are asked to stand in a circle and the facilitators demonstrate the song for the teens. Go over the song a couple of times, and then have everyone sing it together.

> *Lean on me, when you're not strong*
> *I'll be your friend, I'll help you carry on*
> *For, it won't be long*
> *'Til I'm gonna need, somebody to lean on.*
> *You just call on me brother, when you need a friend*
> *We all need somebody to lean on.*
> *I just might have a problem that you'd understand*
> *We all need somebody to lean on.*
> *(repeat first 4 lines)*
> *(Withers, 1972)*

After the opening song, the teens should sit on the carpet in a circle. Teens introduce themselves by saying their name and who died. Explain, "We will be together for the next nine weeks. We will meet for 90 minutes in the same room each week."

Getting To Know Each Other*

Materials
    Markers
    Crayons
    Puzzle pieces
    (See Appendix 2 for sample puzzle pieces)

Say, "Now we will spend some time getting to know each other with these puzzle pieces." Have each teen put his or her name on one of the pieces. Then have the teens draw various things about themselves on their piece. Facilitators should do this activity, too.

Suggestions of possible things for them to draw on their puzzle pieces and share:
Name
Favorite color
Something they like to do for fun
Favorite TV show
A food they hate
What they like to be called
Best friend's name
Something that "bugs" them

Once everyone has shared what they have drawn on their puzzle pieces, explain that all of the pieces are part of a puzzle. Teens are asked to put the puzzle together. The puzzle will be in the shape of a heart. Explain that when a special person dies, some people say they have a broken heart. "We have come into the group to heal our hearts. We are here to share our story with each other and to support each other. In order to put the puzzle together we needed each one of the pieces. That is how it is for our group, too. We need for all of you to support each other. No one person stands alone; just as each puzzle piece cannot stand alone. The puzzle pieces are connected to each other; so are we. We are all connected because each one of us has had a special person die. There are many ways that we are different from each other. But there is one way we are all alike. We have all had a special person die. Sometimes when people have a special person die, they feel alone. The puzzle reminds you that you are not alone and that over the next nine weeks we will be together in this room to help each other out and to share our thoughts and feelings around the death of our special person. Tonight we are going to talk about the death."

Code of Safety*

Materials
Markers
Tagboard

Explain, "We are now going to talk about a Code of Safety. Does anyone know what a Code of Safety is? A Code of Safety is the rules of the group. We need a Code of Safety so that our group can run more smoothly and so that we can trust each other and feel safe. We will be talking about things that may not be very easy to talk about. In order for you to be able to share what you're thinking and feeling, we need to find ways for us all to feel safe enough to do that. Let's try to think of what our group needs to make everyone feel safe in here each week. Does anyone have any ideas?" Here, help the teens come up with ideas by asking them specific questions:

Would you feel safe in here if you were sharing part of your story and other people were talking at the same time?
Would you feel safe in here if you were forced to talk?

Would you feel safe in here if you thought other people in the group told their friends, family members, or other people about your story?

Would you feel safe in here if other people put you down for the things you say and believe?

Is it okay for people to swear in our group? Hit in our group? Invade someone else's personal space? (Share what is meant by "personal space.")

Would you feel safe in here if you thought that everything you said would be shared with your parent or guardian by one of the facilitators?

Here share the limits of confidentiality. "We are required by law to report something you say in the group if we have reason to believe that you might hurt someone else, we have reason to believe that you might hurt yourself, or we have reason to believe that you are being physically or sexually abused. If we think we need to talk to your caregiver about something, we will let you know that first. You can trust that we will not talk about you behind your back."

As the teens answer each of the above questions about feeling safe, help them form a statement that can be written down on the tagboard. In order for it to be written on the tagboard, everyone must agree. "Let's try to think of other ways to keep you safe." All of the teen's suggestions should be incorporated in the Code of Safety.

Examples of what might be written:
    What is said in the group stays in the group
    Everyone has the right to be heard
    Everyone has the right not to talk
    We treat everyone with respect (no hitting, putdowns, etc.)
    Be on time to the group

Once the Code of Safety is written, the teens (and facilitators) sign it. When they sign it, they are promising each other that they will abide by the codes they have agreed on. Spend some time explaining that if someone is disruptive in the group and is preventing others from participating in the group, then that person will be removed from the group until he or she decides to act more appropriately. Three such removals warrant a phone call to the caregiver.

Sharing Feelings (Check-In)*

Materials
    Check-in sheets
    Pencils
    (See Appendix 2 for a sample Check-in sheet)

Explain 'check-in': "A check-in is a time each week when we 'check in' with each other to see how we are feeling." Ask the teens to put a mark on the check-in sheet that depicts how they are feeling on a range from 1–10.

Before the check-in, explain, "There is another way that we can keep you safe.

There may be times in the group when you may be hearing parts of someone else's story that may be hard for you to hear. Or, there may be times when you don't want to share something about your own story. Or, you may want to continue sharing something and the group needs to move on to another activity. We want you to be in control of your story at all times. We want you to feel safe and we want the person who needs to share to feel safe. We want all of you to have an escape plan. That means that you can have a way to escape so that you can keep yourself feeling safe. So one of the ways we can make sure that both things happen is to have you give one of the facilitators a signal. Go over the following scenarios.

> A teen finds it too hard to hear some of the things someone else is saying about his or her story
> A teen has a need to keep talking about something and the other group members are having a hard time hearing some parts of the story
> The group needs to move on so everyone can have a turn
> A teen doesn't want to share any more parts of his or her story

"If you are listening to someone else's story and it is too hard for you to hear some parts of it, the signal will mean that you need to escape for a few moments. One of the facilitators will take you to another room and talk about your feelings and reactions. The rest of the group can stay. If you are sharing part of your story and you don't want to go on any further, you can signal to stop. If you have a need to say more but the group needs to move on, you can signal and one of the facilitators will go to another room with you so you can continue to talk. What do you think of the three escape plans? Will that work for our group? Will that help to make you feel safe? Does anyone have any questions about the three escape plans?" Give the teens a few minutes to think of a signal. Each teen then gives the facilitator their signal.

Now the teens show what number they marked on the check-in sheet. They should say the number they chose and why, and then what special person died, how they died, and when they died. Give each teen a folder in which they can put their check-in sheets and all handouts, and other papers in the sessions.

Introduction to the Topic: What Does "Grief" Mean?*

Materials
Handout: Grief Keys
(See Appendix 2)

Give teens a brief overview of what the group will be doing over the next nine weeks by showing them the Grief Keys handout.

Ask, "Does anyone know what grief is? Grief is all of the thoughts, feelings, and reactions we have when a special person dies."

"Grief Keys are used to help us with our grief as we move through life and experience different kinds of losses. If we put those losses away and never let ourselves grieve them, the thoughts, feelings, and reactions we have around each of these losses never get expressed and then we take them into the next loss. Then when we grieve that loss our grief is bigger than it needs to be."

"Grief Keys help us in two ways: First they help us to keep the feelings about the loss of our special person unlocked so that we keep ourselves in touch with our grief. Second, grief keys are all of the things we can do that will help us with our grief. They are called 'keys' because grief can be difficult, however if we can remember some key things, we can grieve in a healthy way."

"The questions in the middle are all of the questions we need to answer when we have a loss, and ones that we will try to answer over the next nine weeks. The suggestions on the right are all of the things we can do to help us with our grief. Each one of the Grief Keys will be addressed in one of the sessions in the series—each week we will focus on one of these keys. We believe that these five keys can help you with your grief."

"Tonight we will focus on the first key: Getting the Facts." Teens put handouts in their folders.

Telling the Stories: Who Died?/How Did They Die?*

Materials
  Koosh® Ball
  Story cards
  (See Appendix 2 for story cards)

Explain, "We are going to tell a little bit more about our stories." Toss a Koosh® ball to one of the teens and ask a question from one of the story cards. Once that teen has answered the question, he or she tosses the ball to another teen and asks him or her a question on one of the story cards and so on until all of the cards have been used. Note similarities in the teen's experiences as a means of facilitating connections among teens in the group. Remind the teens that they can share as much or as little as they want about their stories. There may be some cards drawn that the teens don't want to answer just yet. For this reason, they can discard up to two cards and ask for another question.

Some of the questions on the cards are:
  Did you know the person was going to die?
  Who told you about the death? What did the person say? What have you been told about what happened?
  How did you feel when you found out that your special person died?
  What do you remember about the last time you saw your special person alive?
  Were you there when your special person died? What was that like?
  Did you get to see the body? What was it like seeing the body?
  Where is your special person now?

After each teen has had a turn, check how the other teens are doing, so as not to traumatize them. Other teens may want to ask questions. The teen telling the story can choose to share only those pieces of the story that he or she wants to tell. After each teen has had a turn to tell his or her story, applaud the teens for their courage. Their stories may be very traumatic and the facilitators want to remind the teens that they have control over how much or how little they want to share with the others. Facilitators remind the teens that it is their hope that the group will be a safe place for them to explore the painful loss of their special person. "In order for it to become safe we need to learn how to trust each other. If we follow our Code of Safety we will have a group that will feel safe for everyone."

Journal Drawing*

Materials
Crayons
Drawing sheets: This is what I Remember about the Funeral and
    This is what I Remember about the Day my Special Person Died
(See Appendix 2 for drawing sheets)

"We have talked a lot about the death and the funeral tonight. Each week we are going to add to our journal at the end of group. Tonight we are going to draw either what you remember about the funeral or what you remember about the death. You can choose which one you want to draw." Pass out the paper and let each teen pick out a comfortable spot in the room to draw his or her picture. When all teens are finished, those who feel comfortable may share what they have drawn. Tell teens, "Next week we will talk more about the funeral."

Closing*

Materials
Affirmations
Affirmation jar
Candle, matches
Resource list
(See Appendix 2 for sample affirmations and resource list)

Each week, the teens sit in a circle around a lit candle; turn the lights in the room off. Explain, "The flame on the candle reminds us of our special person who died. It also reminds us of why we are here in the group." Give the group feedback about how the group went. Give positive reinforcement, for example, noting how well everyone listened, giving appreciation of their courage in sharing their stories, and expressing general enthusiasm about coming weeks. Teens can then pick one of the affirmations from the affirmation jar and read it out loud. Each week they will pick another affirmation. They can take their affirmation home. Remind them to say their affirmation to themselves every day until the group meets again. Ask the teens how the group was for them.

    Remind the teens, "Telling our story can be very hard because it might stir up all of the painful feelings we have around the death. Some of these feelings might stay with you as you leave the group tonight and maybe even into tomorrow. Remember to take care of yourselves. Sharing your thoughts and feelings with a person you trust can be helpful. We all need to share our story with others who can support us. That's why we are here in this group."

"Tonight we talked about the first grief key: Getting the Facts. Remember that if there are any questions you have about the death or anything that continues to concern you, you should talk to someone you know and trust who can answer your questions or help you with your concerns." Pass out a resource list for the teens. Some time should be spent talking about when it might be appropriate to call one of the numbers on the list and when to seek out community resources. Teens should take these resource lists home with them. Tell the teens, "Next week we will explore the word 'death.'"

See Appendix 3 for a sample note given to caregivers each session.

Week 3: Exploring Death

At the beginning of this session the teens are introduced for the first time to the concept of centering. Centering may be unlike anything they have experienced before. For this reason, it may be difficult to convey to the teens the need to be quiet and still. Helping the teens to benefit from the full participation in a centering will take time and patience. One of the facilitators should narrate the centering while the other one models for the teens the kinds of behaviors that are expected for a centering.

This session builds on the concepts introduced in the second session, including continuing to talk about the first grief key: Getting the Facts. The teens are introduced to what it means to be dead and explore basic death concepts including "every living thing dies," "death is not contagious," and "death is irreversible." The concept of "dead" is explored with the teens since it is believed to be central to the weeks that follow. Death is a concrete term and in the context of the group it is explained alone, unconnected to a certain set of spiritual beliefs. Spiritual aspects of death are better left to the teen's family to explain. When teens volunteer information about spiritual beliefs, acknowledge that every family has its own beliefs about death and that those beliefs may be different than other families. Give the teen a simple, straightforward definition of death so that he or she has a good understanding of basic death concepts. The teens do activities where they explore and share their personal beliefs about death. They begin the journal writing, something that they will do each week.

Objectives

To continue the discussion on death
To depict death in a drawing
To explore each teen's personal beliefs around death

Materials

Adjective list
Affirmations
Affirmation jar
Beads
Candle
Cassette or CD player, soft music
Centering activity overview
Centering candle
Code of safety
Crayons
Death art

Drawing sheet: This is what Death Looks Like to Me
Feeling faces sheet
Folders
Funeral photos
Handout: Grief Keys
Journal sheet #1
Matches
Pencils
What I Think About Death cards

Procedures

Note: A star (*) by an activity denotes that this is a main activity, considered central to the session. Unstarred activities are supplemental activities.

Opening Activity*

Materials
   Code of safety

Use the same procedures outlined in Week 2. Remind teens of the Code of Safety and review it with them, then ask if anyone wants to add or take away anything.

Centering Activity*

Materials
   Centering activity overview
   Centering candle, matches
   (See Appendix 2 for the centering activity overview)

Teens are invited to find a place to lay or sit on the floor where they are not touching anyone. The facilitator lights the centering candle and places it near him or her for this activity. One of the facilitators narrates the centering activity, using a soft voice. Other facilitators model for the teens what to do during a centering exercise. The lights in the room should be dimmed or off for this activity. Facilitator reads the overview.

Sharing Feelings (Check-In)*

Materials
   Feeling faces sheet
   Pencils
   (See Appendix 2 for a sample feeling faces sheet)

Teens circle the feeling face that best represents how they are feeling tonight. They share with each other what face they circled and why. When teens check in, they are asked to share one piece of information about the death of their special person that they did not reveal the week before. Compare how everyone is feeling in a general way. The completed feeling faces sheet can go in the teens' folders.

Introduction to the Topic: Exploring Death*

Materials
   Code of safety
   Handout: Grief Keys
   (See Appendix 2 for handout)

Explain that tonight the group is going to continue to talk about death. "We are still talking about the first grief key: Getting the Facts. It is important to get the facts so that we can understand how our special person died." Review the Code of Safety that the group agreed upon last week.

Explain, "Tonight we are going to continue the discussion we had last week. Tonight we are going to focus on the topic of death. It is important that we learn how to understand death so that we don't have to be afraid of it."

"Sometimes we are surrounded by things on TV, radio, movies, or books, that give us the wrong information about the death." Give each teen the opportunity to answer one of the following questions.

> What words do you think of when you think of the word "dead?"
> What symbols come to mind when you think of "dead"?
> What happens to the body when someone dies?
> > The body stops working, the heart doesn't beat, the person doesn't breathe, they don't blink their eyes, they don't feel any more pain, they stop growing, they stay dead, and so forth.
> Can anyone think of a fairy tale that gives us the wrong information about death? Anything on TV? In the movies?
> Ask the children to pay attention to things they hear or see in the next week that give them wrong information about death.

"Death is a natural part of life but most of us don't talk about death and what it means. Anything we don't talk about often becomes something we fear. We fear death because we don't talk about it and we don't know much about it. It is a mystery and it is an unknown. But remember that death is a part of life, everyone dies, death is irreversible, and death is not contagious. People die for a variety of reasons: illness, accidents, murder, suicide, old age."

This is What I Think About Death*

Materials
"What I Think About Death" Cards
(See Appendix 2)

Teens sit in a circle and take turns picking a card out of the stack. Whatever card they pick, they read that statement and say what they think. The object of this exercise is to find out what the teens are thinking about the death. Its purpose is to provide a forum for them to talk about their own personal beliefs about death. Help teens clarify some of the confusing concepts. Other concepts really have no answers. They are a matter of personal beliefs. If a teen does not like the card he or she has drawn he or she may only choose another card once during this exercise.

Funeral Photos

Materials
Funeral photos
(See Appendix 2)

Spread out the different photos of things commonly associated with a funeral face down on the floor (i.e., caskets, cemeteries, tombstones, a church, urn, etc.). Tell teens that these pictures might remind them of the funeral. Teens take turns picking up a photo. When they pick their picture, they are to show the group what picture they have chosen. Then the facilitator asks, "Have you seen what is in the picture? Where? When? Have any of the others? What was that like?"

Other teens in the group are encouraged to talk about the picture. Keep going until everyone has had a turn picking a picture. After each teen has had a turn, ask the teens if they have any questions about the funeral, and if there is anything that they don't understand. Attempt to answer their questions.

Drawing

Materials
Crayons
Death art
Drawing sheet: This is what Death Looks Like to Me
(See Appendix 2 for drawing sheet)

"We've talked a lot about death today. We've talked about how most of us fear death. Let's look at some pictures of how artists have depicted death through the ages." As teens look at the pictures, ask the following questions:

What are the artists saying about death in the pictures?
How do you feel when you look at the pictures?

"Many artists depict death as something to be feared. Remember since death has been a taboo topic, it has been feared through the ages. Now it is your turn to draw your picture of death. Remember, there is no right or wrong way to draw the picture since it comes from your imagination."

After teens have drawn their pictures, have them show them and talk about them. If they don't feel comfortable showing their drawing, have them talk about it.

Journal Writing*

Materials
Adjective list
Beads
Cassette or CD player, soft music
Journal sheet #1
Pencils
(See Appendix 2 for a sample adjective list and journal sheet #1)

"Each week at the end of group we are going to spend some time doing some journal writing. This is a time to think about what we've talked about each night." Go over the journal sheet with the teens before they begin. Encourage the teens to spread out throughout the room to do their journal writing. Play soft music in the background. Completed journal sheets are put in the teens' folders.

During this series, the group members will be making a bead wristband, based on their journal sheets that, when completed, will tell their stories. When the teens fill out the journal sheets with information about a topic, they will also select beads (as indicated on the journal sheets) that depict different things. Usually the colors of the beads that they pick are symbolic of something they have talked about in the session and written about on their journal sheets. You should have the beads available for them to look at so that they can pick out the colors they want each week. They will not actually take the beads or bead their wristband until the ninth session.

Tonight, the teens fill out the first journal sheet. Also, tonight teens are given an adjective list to help them with words that describe themselves, as asked for on the first journal sheet.

Closing*

Materials
    Affirmations
    Affirmation jar
    Candle, matches
    (See Appendix 2 for affirmations)

Use the same procedures outlined in Week 2.

"Remember that although death may seem scary to us because we don't understand it, death is a part of life. All living things die. The more we talk about our questions and our fears, the more information we can get so that we don't have to be afraid. Next week we will talk about the third grief key: Identifying Changes."

■ Week 4: Identifying Changes

This session addresses the myriad of changes that occur after the death of a special person. Teens are especially sensitive to the changes in a home after a death, as often the family structure or responsibilities change. In addition, teens may experience problems with their peer group as they grieve. Although death is a concrete subject and understood by most teens, some may not make the connection between the death and the changes that they are experiencing and feeling. This session helps them to make that connection. The teens are introduced to the concept of change as they explore the world around them and the things that change in nature and in their daily lives.

The facilitator presents aspects of change as they relate to the death of a special person. The teens identify things that they can and cannot change. The session also explores changes in grief reactions over time. The teens are given an opportunity to identify the changes in their own families and in themselves since the death. In this way, the session helps to define for them not only the global changes that are part of all human experience, but also the profound life altering changes that come with the death of a special person in their own lives.

Objectives

To define the word change
To identify different types of change
To identify changes in the family (or friends) since the loss
To identify personal changes since the loss

Materials

Affirmations
Affirmation jar
Beads
Candle
Cassette or CD player, soft music
Centering activity overview
Centering candle
Change cards
Colored die
Crayons

Drawing sheet: Me Before/
   After the Death
Feeling circle
Folders
Grief reaction cards
Handout: Grief Keys
Journal sheet #2
Matches
Pencils
Play-doh®

Procedures

Note: A star (*) by an activity denotes that this is a main activity, considered central to the session. Unstarred activities are supplemental activities.

Opening Activity*

Use the same procedures outlined in Week 2.

Centering Activity*

Materials
Centering activity overview
Centering candle, matches
(See Appendix 2 for the centering activity overview)

Use the same procedures outlined in Week 3.

Sharing Feelings (Check-In)*

Materials
Crayons
Feeling circle
(See Appendix 2 for sample feeling circle)

Teens fill in the feeling circle for check-in this week. Teens are asked to think about how they are feeling right at this moment. Teens are asked to divide up the circle into parts reflecting their feelings. For example, if the teen is feeling very sad and a little confused, he or she will divide the circle into two parts, with the biggest part depicting sad and the smaller part depicting confused. Encourage them to choose different colors to represent different feelings, or they can use shapes to depict the feelings. Once they have completed their circles, have them talk about what they drew as a way to check in. This handout can be put in their folders.

Introduction To The Topic: What Is Change?*

Materials
Handout: Grief Keys
(See Appendix 2)

"Tonight we will talk about another grief key: Identifying Changes. We will try to answer some of the questions on the right of the Grief Keys sheet. "What is change? Change means that something is different. Life has lots of changes. There are things that change everyday. Can you think of things that change? (weather, time, season, feelings, people.) Is all change good? Is all change bad? Is it possible for a family to never change? The hard part about change is that it is different and sometimes that can be scary. Or, it can be sad because we wish that things could be the way they were before. When a special person dies, there can be many changes. Our families and friends change and we can change."

Change Cards*

Materials
>Change cards
>Play-doh®
>(See Appendix 2 for change cards)

Explain that when a special person dies, there can be lots of changes in a family. "We are going to take turns picking a card from the change cards. You should read it out loud and say whether you have experienced that change since the death." Teens sit in a circle and take turns picking a change card. After the teen has responded, ask if other teens have experienced this change. "How did it used to be for you? How is it now? Is this change hard for you and how? Is this change better for you?" Teens may work with Play-doh® during the discussion to help relieve some anxiety they might be experiencing.

Drawing

Materials
>Crayons
>Drawing sheet: Me Before/After the Death
>(See Appendix 2 for drawing sheet)

Facilitator explains that now the teens will spend some time drawing pictures of themselves before and after the death. Reinforce that the death of a special person changes us on a personal level. "Think about what you looked like before the death and what you look like now. If you don't want to draw yourself as a person, you may choose anything that might symbolize what you looked like before the death and then after the death, such as a tree or an animal." What kind of tree or animal were they before the death? What kind of tree or animal are they now? Are they the same tree or animal? If so, how have they changed? Then have them draw that. After they have drawn their pictures have them talk about the pictures they have drawn. If they do not want to show their picture to others in the group, have them talk about what they drew. Drawings are put in the teens' folders.

Common Grief Reactions*

Materials
>Colored die
>Grief reaction cards
>(See Appendix 2 for grief reaction cards)

Explain that when a special person dies, several reactions happen. "We're going to spend some time talking about these reactions now. All of these reactions are normal after a special person dies." Teens take turns tossing a die. Whatever color is tossed, they pick a card that corresponds to the color and read the reaction. Then the teen has to say whether he or she has experienced this reaction since the death. Ask others if they have experienced that reaction. Keep a tally of the various reactions to use upon completing the exercises as a way of showing the teens that these reactions are normal. (Have a tally board where all the teens can see it). If the death occurred some months previously, have the teen try to remember if they experienced this reaction right after the death. One of the colors refer to cards that show reactions that indicate warning signs that they need to pay attention to and get support for.

Once all of the cards have been drawn, reinforce how common these reactions are by sharing how many people in the group endorsed some of the reactions. Remind the teens that these reactions are normal and they will get better with time and will go away. "We have these reactions because of the loss of our special person."

Journal Writing*

Materials
Beads
Cassette or CD player, soft music
Journal sheet #2
Pencils
(See Appendix 2 for journal sheet)

Use the same procedures outlined in Week 3.

Closing*

Materials
Affirmations
Affirmation jar
Candle, matches
(See Appendix 2 for affirmations)

Use the same procedures outlined in Week 2.

"Tonight we talked about the third grief key: Identifying Changes. Remember that change may happen for a long time. As you grow you will change and so will your family or friends. Some things your family or friends used to do, you may do again, some things not. Sometimes, families or friends try new things, sometimes not. But when a special person dies, your family or friends change because that person is no longer with them or you. The important thing to remember is to talk to someone you know and trust about these changes and how these changes make you feel, especially if these changes make you upset. "

"Next week we would like for each of you to bring a picture of your special person who died and something that reminds you of him or her." (Include this information on the note that is sent home to caregivers.)

Week 5: Memories/Remembering

This session helps teens get in touch with the memories they have of their special people. Teens are asked to bring in a picture and something that reminds them of their special person. This activity is the centerpiece of the session. The teens share what they have brought with the group. A memory game and ceremony also reinforce the importance of teen's memories of their special people. The teens do various activities to remember and share different memories, and they write in their journals. Lastly, the remembrance ceremony is used to illustrate that even though the teens have lost the physical presence of their special person in their lives, they can still remember them in their hearts; that part of them will never go away.

Objectives

To define the word "memory"
To discuss the importance of memories
To share pictures and belongings of the special person
To recall good memories

Materials

Affirmations
Affirmation jar
Beads
Candle
Cassette or CD player, soft music
Centering activity overview
Centering candle
Check-in sheets
Crayons

Drawing sheet: My Best Memory
Folders
Handout: Grief Keys
Journal sheet #3
Matches
Memory cards
Pencils
Pictures/belongings of special people
Tea lights (1 for each child)

Procedures

Note: A star (*) by an activity denotes that this is a main activity, considered central to the session. Unstarred activities are supplemental activities.

Opening Activity*

Use the same procedures outlined in Week 2.

Centering Activity*

Materials
Centering activity overview
Centering candle, matches
(See Appendix 2 for the centering activity overview)

Use the same procedures outlined in Week 3.

Sharing Feelings (Check-In)*

Materials
Check-in sheets
Pencils
(See Appendix 2 for sample check-in sheets)

Teens mark an 'X' on the Check-in sheet that shows how they are feeling tonight. They share with each other how they are feeling. Sheets are put into the teens' folders

Introduction To The Topic: What Is A Memory?*

Materials
Handout: Grief Keys
(See Appendix 2)

"Tonight we will talk about the second grief key: remembering/memories. We will try to answer some of the questions on the right. What is a memory? A memory is something we remember about something, someone, or something we did. Why are memories important when a special person dies? Because they are no longer with us. Memories help us to remember that person. It's the part of the person that doesn't go away. Even though their body is no longer with us—we cannot hug them, touch them, or hear them—we can still remember them. It's important to talk about them and remember the person who died so that we don't forget them. Some memories are pleasant, like if we hear a song or go somewhere we went with the special person or see something that the person gave us. Not all memories are pleasant. Some memories may be unpleasant, particularly around the death, or a time when you argued with your special person. Tonight we will spend the entire evening talking about memories."

Sharing Our Memories*

Materials
Pictures/belongings of special people

Teens share with other group members the pictures and personal belongings they brought, or other personal belongings that remind them of their special person. Teens can pass around the things that they have brought if they want, but they don't have to. They should be reminded to take special care of other people's things because they are special memories of a special person. After all of the teens have shared, thank the teens for bringing in their memories and sharing and for taking special care of each others' memories.

Memory Cards*

Materials
    Memory cards
    (See Appendix 2)

"Now we will spend some time sharing memories of our special people." Teens take turns drawing a memory card and remembering something on the card; for example, they might remember a birthday or holiday spent with the special person. Teens share aloud with the group. Others may respond to any particular memory. Teens continue to take turns picking cards until all of the cards have been chosen.

Drawing

Materials
    Crayons
    Drawing sheet: My Best Memory
    (See Appendix 2 for drawing sheet)

"Now I want you to think about one of the best memories you have of your special person and draw it." Once teens have drawn their pictures, have them show or talk about them with the group. They can then put these in their folders.

Journal Writing*

Materials
    Beads
    Cassette or CD player, soft music
    Journal sheet #3
    Pencils
    (See Appendix 2 for journal sheet)

Use the same procedures outlined in Week 3.

Closing*

Materials
Affirmations
Affirmation jar
Candle, matches
Tea lights (1 for each child)
(See Appendix 2 for affirmations)

Each group member is given a tea light. A center candle is lit. "Tonight we are going to light a candle in memory of your special person." Each teen goes to the center candle to light his or her candle and share one thing he or she remembers about the special person. Reinforce that memories are important because they will always stay with the teen as long as he or she keeps those memories in his or her heart and mind. Teens can take their tea lights home with them to burn in memory of their special people. "Some ways that we can do the second grief key is to continue to talk about and remember the special person who died and ask others who knew them to tell us about what they remember."

"Next week we will talk about feelings."

Week 6: Identifying and Expressing Feelings

The goal for this session is two-fold: to help the teens identify and label their feelings around the death and to validate their feelings. Through 'check-in' the teens have learned by now how to label the four basic feelings. Now they are being asked to relate these feelings to their experience of the death. No judgments are made about the feelings that they have or how they express them. Here, the focus of the session is only to identify and label the feelings and to talk about how they express them. In this way, they can make the connection between their feelings and the death as well as the feelings of others around them and the death.

Objectives

> To define feelings
> To identify different feelings and how they are manifested
> To identify feelings around death

Materials

Affirmations
Affirmation jar
Beads
Candle
Cassette or CD player, soft music
Centering activity overview
Centering candle
Crayons
Drawing sheet: Something That Makes Me Mad, Sad, Scared, and Happy

Feeling faces sheet
Feelings of grief list
Fight and flight cards
Folders
Handout: Grief Keys
Journal sheet #4
Matches
Pencils

Procedures

Note: A star (*) by an activity denotes that this is a main activity, considered central to the session. Unstarred activities are supplemental activities.

*Opening Activity**

Use the same procedures outlined in Week 2.

Centering Activity*

Materials
Centering activity overview
Centering candle, matches
(See Appendix 2 for the centering activity overview)

Use the same procedures outlined in Week 3.

Sharing Feelings (Check-In)*

Materials
Feeling faces sheet
Pencils
(See Appendix 2 for the feeling faces sheet)

Teens pick out a feeling face that depicts how they are feeling today. The sheets then go into their folders.

Introduction To The Topic: What are Feelings?*

Materials
Handout: Grief Keys
(See Appendix 2 for feeling photos and handouts)

"Tonight and next week we will talk about the fourth grief key: Expressing Feelings. We will try to answer the questions on the right hand side of the sheet."

Ask, "What is a feeling?" Let teens offer suggestions and then elaborate by saying, "A feeling is something that we think or react to, and it makes us act a certain way. Ask teens to name some feelings. Explain that sometimes it is possible to tell what someone is feeling by their behavior, but remind them that all people don't act the same way even if they are feeling the same feeling.

"Do all of your family members (or friends) feel the same way about the special person who died? Is it possible for people in the same family (or friends) to feel different feelings all at the same time."

Summarize this discussion in this way:
Everyone has feelings
People express their feelings in different ways
We may not always be able to "see" how someone is feeling
It's okay to have feelings—all feelings
If we don't express our feelings, it can make us tired, we can get sick, or it may come out in different ways.

Feeling Sentence Starters*

Materials
   Feeling sentence starters
   (See Appendix 2)

Teens and facilitators each pick four sentence starter cards. They should read each one to themselves. Explain to the teens that they need to complete at least three of the sentences (i.e., "When I am happy . . . " I smile and laugh a lot). Then go around the group having each person respond, taking turns completing one card per turn. Keep going until all of the teens and facilitators have responded to three cards each.

Fight and Flight Cards*

Materials
   Fight and Flight Cards
   (See Appendix 2)

"When we grieve it is very hard for us to let ourselves feel the painful feelings. So most of us use two methods to try to push down the pain, until we feel ready to let ourselves feel the pain. The first way we try to cope with our feelings is to fight our feelings. We think if we try hard enough we can keep our grief away. So we spend a lot of energy running from our pain. We keep ourselves busy and never slow down long enough to let ourselves feel anything. The second way we try to cope with our feelings is that we flee our feelings. We think if we ignore our feelings and pretend that we're not all that upset we won't have to feel any pain. So we don't spend much time or energy allowing ourselves to feel our feelings. We try to escape our feelings. We're going to see how you cope with your feelings. Remember, most everyone uses both of these techniques until they feel ready to feel the pain of their grief. Let's see if you use both techniques or mostly one."

Teens are asked to pick a card from the fight and flight pile of cards. They are to read each card out loud and say whether each one is a coping technique they use. If they don't use that technique, they put the card at the bottom of the appropriate pile. If they do, they keep the card. Then the next teen takes a turn and so on until all of the cards are gone. Once the group has gone through all of the cards, the facilitator asks the teens to count how many fight and flight cards they have. Do they have more of one type of card, or are their piles equally balanced? If they have many more cards of one category, it may mean that they are using this technique too much and they need to pay attention to that. Sometimes these coping techniques can turn into a defense, preventing teens from feeling their feelings and not allowing them to grieve.

Drawing

Materials
> Crayons
> Drawing sheet: Something That Makes Me Mad, Sad, Scared, and Happy
> (See Appendix 2 for drawing sheet)

"I would like you to think of the feelings you have or have had since the death. Now we're going to draw something that makes you or has made you feel mad, sad, scared, and happy since the death of your special person." After the pictures are drawn on the sheet, teens can show or talk about their pictures with the group. Drawings are put into their folders.

*Journal Writing**

Materials
> Beads
> Cassette or CD player, soft music
> Feelings of grief list
> Journal sheet #4
> Pencils
> (See Appendix 2 for feelings of grief list and journal sheet)

Use the same procedures outlined in Week 3. In addition, each teen is given a feelings of grief list to help him or her identify 'feeling' words.

*Closing**

Materials
> Affirmations
> Affirmation jar
> Candle, matches
> (See Appendix 2 for affirmations)

Use the same procedures outlined in Week 2.

"Tonight we learned lots of things about feelings. What are some of the things we learned? This is a very important grief key. If we don't express our feelings around the death, they can build up. That's why it's important to learn ways to express our feelings." Next week we will talk about Unfinished Business."

◼ Week 7: Exploring Unfinished Business

This session focuses on unfinished business. The activities of this session will help the teens to understand what is meant by unfinished business. Some younger teens may not be able to explore this topic to the depth of older teens or their caregivers, but they can understand the sense of responsibility they may feel for the death of their special person; they therefore need to be reassured that they had nothing to do with the death. One activity explores what the teens may think they did to cause the death, things they may blame themselves for, or things they think they could have done to prevent the death. The teens symbolically let these thoughts go. Teens may draw or write about the last memory they have of their special person and share it with the group, exploring anything that still bothers them about the death, including any remaining guilt they may have. At the end of the session the teens write a love note to their special person, saying anything that they would like to say to them. A note is sent home with the caregivers explaining the love notes and how they can help the teens decide what to do with them. This activity draws the caregiver into the teen's need to communicate with his or her special person and helps the caregivers to understand the importance of keeping that link for the teen.

Objectives

To define unfinished business and learn four ways that it can affect teen's ability to grieve the death of their special person
To discuss the things the teens didn't get to do with their special person
To say what the teens didn't get to say to their special person
To share anything about the death that remains troubling

Materials

Affirmations
Affirmation jar
Bowl (to burn post-its in)
Candle
Centering activity overview
Centering candle
Coulda-woulda-shoulda Post-it notes
Crayons

Drawing sheet: My Last Memory
Feeling faces sheet
Folders
Handout: Grief Keys
Love notes
Matches
Pencils
Tea lights (or small candle)

Procedures

Note: A star (*) by an activity denotes that this is a main activity, considered central to the session. Unstarred activities are supplemental activities.

Opening Activity*

Use the same procedures outlined in Week 2.

Centering Activity*

Materials
Centering activity overview
Centering candle, matches
(See Appendix 2 for the centering activity overview)

Use the same procedures outlined in Week 3.

Sharing Feelings (Check-In)

Materials
Feeling faces sheet
Pencils
(See Appendix 2 for sample feeling faces sheet)

For check-in tonight, teens find the face on the sheet that is appropriate to how they are feeling. These sheets are then put into their folders

Introduction To The Topic: Exploring Unfinished Business

Materials
Handout: Grief Keys
(See Appendix 2)

"Tonight we are going to talk about when your special person died. How many of you got to say good-bye to your special person before he or she died?" If a teen did, have him or her describe what happened. "Tonight we're going to talk about something called 'unfinished business.' Does anyone know what that means? Unfinished business is anything that prevents you from grieving the loss of your special person. There are lots of things that can prevent us from grieving."

"We're going to talk about how you might feel if you didn't get to say good-bye, if something about the death of your special person still bothers you, if there are things you didn't get to do with your special person, and if people in your families (or friends) don't let you grieve."

Coulda-woulda-shoulda*

Materials

> Bowl (to burn post-its in)
> Coulda-woulda-shoulda post-it notes
> Matches
> Tea light (or small candle)
> Pencils

Put three post-it notes on each of the teens. One says "coulda," one says "woulda," and one says "shoulda." Explain, "Sometimes when someone dies, we think that there must have been something we could have done to prevent his or her death. We may blame ourselves. We think we should have acted differently at the time of his or her death or that some negative thought we had about our special person before he or she died may have caused the death. We call these thoughts coulda-woulda-shouldas. We think to ourselves I coulda. . . . I woulda. . . . I shoulda. . . . and get mad at ourselves. These coulda-woulda-shouldas can stick to us just like the post-its and interfere with our grief because we feel so guilty about something. Let's spend some time thinking about some of the coulda-woulda-shouldas that you have." Teens are asked to take a few minutes to think about the coulda-woulda-shoulda's they have around the death of their special person. Take one phrase at a time and have the teens think about and share their coulda-woulda-shouldas. For example, "I coulda been nicer . . . " "I shoulda called more often . . . " and so on.

As each teen shares they can take that post-it off of themselves. After each teen takes his or her turn, others in the group are encouraged to say something to him or her. This is not intended to talk them out of how they feel, but to empathize and offer encouragement. The action of taking off the post-it symbolizes their willingness not to let it stick to them anymore. Now the teens are asked to think about which coulda-woulda-shouldas they might be open to letting go of and what ones they need to hold onto for now. They are asked to tear up the ones they want to let go of and put them into a bowl. Once they are in a bowl, they should be mixed up. This "mixing up" indicates that no one is more or less guilty than anyone in the group. Burn the torn pieces of paper as a symbol of letting go. Put a small candle in a bowl (ceramic or metal) and then add the post-its to be burned. Then the group should decide as a whole what to do with the ashes. Should they be strewn in the soil to feed a plant, flower, or tree? In this way the group has, as a whole, taken something negative and turned it into a positive.

My Last Memory*

Materials

> Crayons
> Drawing sheet: My Last Memory
> (See Appendix 2 for drawing sheet)

Teens are asked to draw the last memory they have of their special person when he or she was still alive. After they have completed their drawing they can share them with the group. Here is an opportunity to explore anything about the death of their special person that still bothers them including any remaining guilt they may have. Drawings are put into their folders.

Love Notes*

Materials
    Love notes
    Pencils
    (See Appendix 2 for sample love notes)

Facilitator reminds the children about how many of them did not get to say good-bye to their special person. Even if they did, they likely still have things they want to say to their special person. "We're going to think about what we would like to say to our special person and write that on a love note." Teens write down what they would have liked to say. Then the facilitator goes around the circle and asks the children to share what they would have liked to say. Talk to the teens about what they want to do with their love notes. Do they want to take it to the cemetery? Do they want to take it home and put it in a special place? Do they want to have their caregivers read it? Do they want to put it away as something to keep and remember about their special person?

Closing*

Materials
    Affirmations
    Affirmation jar
    Candle, matches
    (See Appendix 2 for affirmations)

Use the same procedures outlined in Week 2.

"Next week we will talk about coping with feelings."

◼ Week 8: Coping With Feelings

This session builds on the concepts presented in Week 6. While that session was intended to help the teens identify and label their feelings and the ways that they express them, this session is intended to help them learn healthy coping techniques. A balloon is used in the session to illustrate in a very concrete way what can happen if the teens don't let their feelings out. The teens also explore how feelings might come out if they are not expressed appropriately. A relaxation activity teaches teens one way to deal with their feelings in a healthy way. They are also taught a technique called thought stopping to help them replace negative thoughts. There is also an activity where they express their sadness through art. They are also given prescriptions for feelings which are suggestions that they can use to make themselves feel better when they are having difficult or hard feelings. Finally, the mad targets help the teens to express their anger. All of the activities are geared to illustrate to the teens how they can cope with feelings in a healthy way.

Facilitators should meet with caregivers individually for about 10–15 minutes before or after this session to discuss the teen's grief and current adjustment. In addition, discuss whether further participation of the youth is recommended or desired. Recommendations may be provided regarding appropriate bereavement services considering the current adjustment of the teen and the primary caregiver's concerns.

Objectives

To identify reactions to feelings
To identify feelings that are troubling
To learn healthy ways to cope with feelings

Materials

Affirmations	Handout: Grief Keys
Affirmation jar	Journal sheet #5
Beads	Mad target
Balloon	Matches
Blank paper	Pencils
Bubble wrap	Plastic sheet
Candle	Play-doh®
Cassette or CD player, soft music	Prescriptions for feelings
Centering candle	Relaxation activity
Crayons	Thought stopping worksheet
Feeling faces sheet	Wet sponges
Folders	

Procedures

Note: A star (*) by an activity denotes that this is a main activity, considered central to the session. Unstarred activities are supplemental activities.

Opening Activity*

Use the same procedures outlined in Week 2.

Centering Activity*

Materials
    Centering candle, matches
    Relaxation activity
    (See Appendix 2 for the relaxation activity)

Tonight, facilitators will follow the same procedures as for the centering activity, however, they will use the relaxation activity instead of the centering activity overview. Emphasize how the centering the group has been doing each week is a way to cope with difficult feelings. Ask, "Do any of you think that you can use this exercise at other times?" Reinforce that using an imagery can sometimes help children fall asleep if they are having a hard time falling or staying asleep.

Sharing Feelings (Check-In)*

Materials
    Feeling faces sheet
    Pencils
    (See Appendix 2 for feeling faces sheet)

For check-in tonight, teens are to indicate all of the feelings they have had since the death of their special person. What feelings do they think the different drawings depict? Circle feelings they have had in the last week. Draw a square around feelings they are feeling tonight. What makes them feel that way? Sheets are put into their folders.

Introduction To The Topic: Coping with Feelings*

Materials
    Balloon
    Handout: Grief Keys
    (See Appendix 2 for handout)

"Tonight we are going to continue talking about the fourth grief key: Expressing Feelings, specifically coping with feelings. "Why is it important to express our feelings?

Because if we don't, they really don't go anywhere, and they will affect us in some way. They will make us tired; they can make us sick or make us overreact." Illustrate this with a balloon. "If we continue to stuff our feelings just as if we continue to add air to the balloon, our feelings will explode just like the balloon. But if we express our feelings and let them out a little at a time, this won't happen." Let the air out of the balloon a little at a time.

"Sometimes when we feel a feeling, we do something to cope with the feeling. What does it mean to cope? Coping means that we do something to help us with the intensity of the feeling. Sometimes people cope with feelings in a healthy way, sometimes not. What might be some ways someone may cope with a feeling in an unhealthy way?" Have teens name some things that might indicate they are not coping with their feelings in a healthy way.

Some possible ideas:
Getting into fights
Withdrawing from family and friends
Overeating or undereating
Keeping too busy
Drugs, alcohol, smoking
Stealing, lying
Keeping feelings bottled up inside and never talking to anyone about them.

"Tonight we are going to learn some ways to help us cope with our feelings in a healthy way."

Coping With Our Feelings in a Healthy Way: Thought-Stopping*

Materials
Pencils
Thought-stopping worksheet
(See Appendix 2 for worksheet)

"There is a way to help us cope with our feelings when they are hard to shake—it's called thought-stopping. Thought-stopping can help us when we get a thought in our head and we can't get it out. These thoughts can make us feel bad about ourselves. When we get a thought like this, we actually can stop the thought. We say to ourselves, 'Stop.' Then we replace that thought with another thought. The new thought helps us to change how we feel. Let's go over this worksheet." Go over the sheet to explain thought stopping. Give teens time to think of ways to use thought stopping for each of the examples before discussing it with the group. Teens keep this worksheet in their folders.

Bubble Wrap

Materials
  Bubble wrap

For fun, each teen gets a piece of bubble wrap to pop!

Draw or Sculpt "Sad"*

Materials
  Blank paper
  Play-doh®
  Crayons

"Sometimes we can't talk about how we feel, but we can express our feelings in other ways. Another way to help us cope with our feelings is to express how we feel through art. Take some time to draw a picture of the feeling, 'sad' or take the Play-doh® and make it look like 'sad.'" After the teens have drawn their pictures or sculpted something for sad, have them share what they have done and explain it to the group. Reinforce that sometimes teens can't talk about how they feel, but they can express their feelings in other ways.

Prescriptions for Feelings

Materials
  Pencils
  Prescriptions for feelings
  (See Appendix 2 for prescriptions for feelings)

"When we get sick we go to the doctor and sometimes he or she gives us a prescription. Do you know what a prescription is? A prescription is a sheet of paper signed by the doctor that you take to a drug store to get some medicine to help you feel better. Tonight we are going to give ourselves prescriptions for feelings. Let's talk about 'sad.'" Have each teen name something that makes him or her feel sad. Then the facilitator goes over the list on their sheets with them (i.e., suggestions for how to make them feel better). Facilitator and teens then think of other ways to cope with their sadness. Teens write down these ideas. Then teens decide on another feeling, write a prescription for that, go over the suggestions on the provided prescriptions, and so on. In this way, the teens will be getting a lot of suggestions for coping with feelings.

Mad Target*

Materials
　Mad target
　Plastic sheet
　Wet sponges

Show the teens the Mad Target. "Sometimes we get angry when we lose someone close to us." "Tonight we are going to get our anger out in a healthy way. Let's think of some things that make us mad. Now we will take turns throwing these wet sponges at the target. Hurl the sponge at the target, shouting, "I am mad at . . . because. . . . !" For example, "I am mad at my dad because he died," "I am mad at my brother because he should have been more careful." Then each teen takes a turn throwing a wet sponge at the target and shouting. Each teen may take several turns. After the exercise facilitators ask the teens how it felt to throw the sponges. How do they feel now? What is something they could do at home that is similar to this exercise that could help them with their anger?

Journal Writing*

Materials
　Beads
　Cassette or CD player, soft music
　Journal sheet #5
　Pencils
　(See Appendix 2 for journal sheet)

Use the same procedures outlined in Week 3.

Closing*

Materials
　Affirmations
　Affirmation jar
　Candle, matches
　Note cards or slips of paper
　(See Appendix 2 for Affirmations)

Use the same procedures outlined in Week 3.

　Tell the children that the group has spent two sessions talking about feelings. Remind the teens, "We don't have to let our feelings rule us, there are many healthy ways to cope with our feelings." Next week we will learn about self-care and support."

　Remind the teens that group pictures will be taken next week.

Week 9: Learning Self-Care and Support

This session covers the concept of self-care and an important aspect of self-care; support. When a family experiences the death of a special person, teens may not receive the same type of care they were used to or they may take on additional responsibilities; thus it is important to teach teens self-care techniques. Time is spent focusing on the importance of self-care including eating right, playing, sleeping well, expressing feelings, and keeping their bodies clean. Through activities, they learn what can happen if they don't have enough support in their lives. The teens play a game that helps them to think about who they can go to for different kinds of support. Even teens this age need help identifying key people in their lives who can give them support. The emphasis during this session is to get them to think about and name these people since they will need them as they move through their mourning.

Group pictures are taken tonight. Each teen will be given a group picture at the last session to remind him or her of the support he or she got in the group.

Facilitators should meet with caregivers individually for about 10–15 minutes before or after this session to discuss the teen's grief and current adjustment. In addition, discuss whether further participation of the youth is recommended or desired. Recommendations may be provided regarding appropriate bereavement services considering the current adjustment of the teen and the primary caregiver's concerns.

Objectives

> To define self-care and support
> To discuss why self-care and support are important
> To learn ways to get support and practice self-care

Materials

Affirmations
Affirmation jar
Beads
Bio-dots®
Bio-dot® cards
Camera with film
Candle
Cassette or CD player, soft music
Centering activity overview
Centering candle
Directions for relaxation and breathing exercises

Elastic (or fishing wire and clasps)
Feeling faces sheet
Folders
Handout: Grief Keys
Matches
Pencils
Problem solving plan handout
Problem solving scenarios
Support wheels

Procedures

Note: A star (*) by an activity denotes that this is a main activity, considered central to the session. Unstarred activities are supplemental activities.

Opening Activity*

Use the same procedures outlined in Week 2.

Centering Activity*

Materials
Centering activity overview
Centering candle, matches
(See Appendix 2 for the centering activity overview)

Use the same procedures outlined in Week 3.

Sharing Feelings (Check-In)*

Materials
Feeling faces sheet
Pencils
(See Appendix 2 for feeling faces sheet)

Teens check-in by selecting a feeling face that signifies how they are feeling tonight. Sheets are then put into their folders.

Introduction To The Topic: Learning Self-Care and Support*

Materials
Handout: Grief Keys
(See Appendix 2)

Explain, "Tonight we are going to talk about self-care and support which are part of the fifth grief key: Finding Help." Introduce the topic of self-care with the following list of questions and comments:

Does anyone know what self-care means?
It means taking care of ourselves: our bodies, our minds, and our feelings so that we can grow up to be healthy and happy. It means thinking thoughts and doing things that are good for us—that make us feel good and help us to stay healthy. There are lots of ways we can take care of our bodies. One way is to eat good food that helps us grow. We can also get enough sleep.
Are there any other ways we can take care of our bodies?
Keep our bodies, hair, and teeth clean, get lots of exercise, and play in the fresh air. There are other ways we can take care of ourselves too. It's important to take care of our feelings as well. When we feel mad, sad, and scared, we need to tell other people how we feel.

"When a special person dies, we need to make sure that we are taking care of ourselves so that we can stay healthy. Another way to use self-care is to get support. Does anyone know what support means? Support means 'help.' All of us need support sometimes. All of us need help sometimes."

Illustrate why teens need support with the help of one of the group members. Ask the teen to lean back and hold him or her up. Ask the teens what would happen if the teen did not have someone to lean on? He or she would fall over because he or she would not have any support. "That's why we need support, because if we try to stand alone without help, we aren't as strong."

"Why do you think self-care and support are so important? With self-care and support, you will eat, sleep, look, and act better. You will be able to stay healthy and get the most out of life."

"Tonight we are going to learn ways to take care of ourselves."

Support Wheel*

Materials
Pencils
Support wheels
(See Appendix 2 for a sample support wheel)

Explain that the group is going to take a look at the support wheel. "Just as a wheel needs all of its spokes in order to roll, so do we need people in our lives for each one of the spokes on our support wheel. Take a few minutes to fill out the support wheel and fill in each spoke with the names of people who can give you that kind of support." After the teens have filled out their sheet have them study it. Are there any spokes that don't have names on them? If so, can they think of someone who might give them that kind of support? Are there only one or two people named on the support wheel? That may mean that they are depending on one person too much. Facilitators remind the teens that each one of these kinds of support is important to them as they grieve the loss of their special person. If they need more support they need to find more people who can give them support.

Problem Solving Plan*

Materials
Problem solving plan handout
Problem solving scenarios
(See Appendix 2 for handout and scenarios)

"We often are confronted with problems in our lives that we don't quite know how to handle. Sometimes we react quickly and end up hurting someone else or getting ourselves into trouble. Today we are going to learn a problem solving plan that can help you with any kind of problem." Go over the problem solving plan handout with the teens. Now ask for volunteers from the group who are dealing with a particular problem in their lives right now. Have the group use the plan to help that group member solve the problem. Use the problem solving scenarios as a back up in case no one volunteers. Remind the teens that they can always use this plan when they have problems. The handout is put into their folders so that they can use it for future reference. Facilitators urge the teens to try to keep practicing the problem solving plan.

Relaxation and Breathing Exercises*

Materials
    Bio-dots®
    Bio-dot® cards
    Directions for relaxation and breathing exercises
    (See Appendix 2 for relaxation and breathing exercise instructions)

Pass out the Bio-dots® and card and explain, "We're going to see how relaxed we are and then by doing different things see if we change the color on the dot." Explain the different colors and what they stand for. Teens put the dot between their pointer finger and their thumb on the fleshy part of the top of their hand. After a minute ask the teens, "What color is the dot now?" Then teens are asked to think of something that makes them angry or upset. "What color does the dot turn?"

Do the relaxation exercise and breathing exercises. Teens should sit in a circle on chairs.

At the end of the exercise, say, "Both of these techniques bring us quick energy." Check to see if their Bio-dots® changed color? Review the information regarding what each color means with the teens (on the back of the card) and encourage them to use it whenever they can. Teens can take their Bio-dot® Card and one Bio-dot® home with them.

Journal Activity*

Materials
    Beads
    Cassette or CD player, soft music
    Journals (Folders)
    Elastic (or fishing wire and clasps)

This week for journal writing, teens bead their wristbands, using the colors of beads that they have been picking each session on their journal sheets. As the teens work on this, the facilitator can walk around and review teen's journal sheets. Teens show their bead wristbands to each other, explaining how the wristbands represent their stories. The teens can take their completed journals and wristbands home with them tonight.

*Closing**

Materials
    Affirmations
    Affirmation jar
    Camera with film
    Candle, matches
    (See Appendix 2 for affirmations)

Use the same procedures outlined in Week 2. The group picture is taken.

    Remind the teens that next week will be the last week of group, and that their caregivers are invited to join the group for the party at the end of the session.

Week 10: Learning to Say Good-Bye

This session helps the teens say good-bye to each other and to the group experience. Another main goal of this session is to bolster their self-esteem. The teens write an affirmation or something that they appreciated about each teen in the group and each teen takes this list home. They also write a letter to future group members with any advice or encouragement that they can offer. The group has a small party and the session is more relaxed than previous sessions. The party and refreshments are intended to create some distance from the heaviness of the preceding weeks as the teens disengage from the group. The teens complete their group evaluations. At the end of the session, the puzzle pieces from the first week are brought out again to talk about the connections that they have with each other. The teens talk about how they have changed, what they have learned, and so forth. Each teen takes the puzzle piece, his or her affirmation list, and a group picture home as reminders of the group experience. They are reminded that they have met other teens just like them, and they have these objects, memories, and connections to comfort them as they continue to mourn after the group has ended.

Objectives

To identify the teen's personal gifts and strengths
To say good-bye to each other
To celebrate the group's last time together

Materials

Affirmations
Affirmation jar
Blank paper
Candle
Centering activity pverview
Centering candle
Childhood Depression Inventory
   (CDI)

Common Grief Reactions Checklist (CGRC)
Group evaluations
Group pictures
Matches
Note cards or slips of paper
Pencils
Puzzle pieces
Snacks

Procedures

Note: A star (*) by an activity denotes that this is a main activity, considered central to the session. Unstarred activities are supplemental activities.

Opening Activity*

Use the same procedures outlined in Week 2.

Centering Activity*

Materials
 Centering activity overview
 Centering candle, matches
 (See Appendix 2 for the centering activity overview)

Use the same procedures outlined in Week 3.

Sharing Feelings (Check-In)*

Teens share how they feel about the group ending.

Introduction To The Topic: Saying Good-Bye*

Explain that tonight is the group's last time together. "Tonight we will be spending time saying good-bye to each other. It's not easy to say good-bye. Some (or all) of you didn't get to say good-bye to your special person. That's why we're going to take time to let you say good-bye to each other."

Group Evaluations*

Materials
 Childhood Depression Inventory (CDI)
 Common Grief Reactions Checklist (CGRC)
 Pencils
 (See Appendix 1 for CDI and Appendix 2 for CGRC)

In this session, facilitators should gather postgroup participation information, including the Childhood Depression Inventory (CDI) and Common Grief Reactions Checklist (CGRC), which were collected at the beginning of the 10 sessions. In addition, the teens should fill out a group evaluation form, which asks them to rate the group on various dimensions such as how much they enjoyed it and how helpful it was. When group members fill out this sheet, leave the room or go to another part of the room so that teens feel comfortable saying what they need to say on the evaluations. Ask for a volunteer to put the evaluations in an envelope and give it to the program director. Information about how to obtain the CDI can be found in Appendix 1.

Affirmation Notes*

Materials
  Blank paper
  Pencils

Each group member writes his or her name at the bottom of a piece of paper and then passes it to the person on his or her left. The person it was passed to writes an encouraging word or something they appreciated about that person. Then the notes are passed again until everyone in the group has written a note to everyone else (including facilitators). Group members take their notes home with them.

Letter Writing*

Materials
  Blank paper
  Pencils

Tonight instead of journal writing, teens are asked to write a letter to other teens who will be coming into a future group. What can they tell them about the group? What words of encouragement do they have for them as they grieve? What advice can they pass on that will help others with their grief? What have they learned about grief from the group that has helped? These letters will then be shared with teens who will be enrolled in future groups. If a teen has completed this activity with a previous group, he or she can read a few of these letters again at this time.

Closing*

Materials
  Affirmations
  Affirmation jar
  Candle, matches
  Group pictures
  Puzzle pieces
  (See Appendix 2 for affirmations)

Facilitators have the teens sit in a circle around the candle. "Ten weeks ago we began our group. We talked about how we are all connected in a special way. Does anyone remember what the connection is? We are connected because we have had a special person die. Remember how we each got a puzzle piece and talked about how we are all connected?" Have teens put the puzzle together again. "We talked about how we needed each puzzle piece to put the puzzle together just as we all needed each other over the last 10 weeks to help each other out. Tonight each one of you will take your puzzle piece with you. Think about how you have changed since the beginning of group. What helped you? What did you learn?" As each teen takes his or her puzzle piece from the puzzle, encourage the teen to share what he or she has learned from the group. "The puzzle piece reminds us that we will always be connected. So whenever you are feeling alone, all you need to do is look at your puzzle piece and remember that you will always be connected to each other." Remind the group that they should continue to think of each other even though the group will end.

Use the same procedures outline in Week 2. A group picture is given to each teen. Teens take home their folders of "journals."

Party Time*

Materials
Snacks

Teens can enjoy a beverage and a snack. Suggestions: crackers, popcorn, juice. Caregivers are welcome to join the group for the party.

Resources

Jimerson, S. (1997). Jimerson—Common Grief Reactions Checklist (CGRC). Available from the author.
Jimerson, S. (1997). Jimerson—Grief Support Groups General Information Sheet (GIS). Available from the author.
Kovacs, M. (1992). The Childhood Depression Inventory (CID). New York: Multi-Health Systems.
Withers B. (1972). Lean on me. Sony Music Entertainment.

A Description of Materials

Note: The materials included with each level of the grief curriculum are designed to be developmentally appropriate; therefore, although the names of the materials may be the same, the materials differ slightly across the curriculum levels.

Adjective List: This list is provided for the teens as they work on the first journal sheet to give them ideas for words that might describe themselves. The adjective list can be found in Appendix 2.

Affirmations: Affirmations are one-sentence statements encouraging positive/affirming thoughts (e.g., My grief is unique. I will let myself grieve in my one way.). The affirmations can be copied onto colorful paper, cut out as strips of paper, and then rolled up (by wrapping them around a pencil) and placed into the affirmation jar (described below). Affirmations are used at the end of each session to provide each member with an affirming thought until the next group meeting. Affirmations can be found in Appendix 2.

Affirmation Jar: The affirmation jar is offered to the teens at the end of every session. Copy the affirmations onto brightly colored or neon copy paper, cut them out, and roll them up. The affirmations are then put into a clear candy jar with a lid. The affirmations look like candy in the jar. At the end of each session, teens are asked to pick an affirmation from the jar and read it out loud. The affirmation jar is intended to bolster the group members' self-esteem which can be so badly damaged after a significant loss in their lives. Affirmations can be found in Appendix 2.

Balloon: The balloon is used to illustrate what can happen if we don't let feelings out. If too much air is put into a balloon, eventually it will pop. But if a little bit of air is let out of the balloon it won't. Similarly, it is possible to prevent exploding by expressing feelings a little bit at a time. Feelings that get expressed prevent people from letting their feelings get out of control. It is best to use a medium size balloon (4–5 inches around). If the balloon is too large, it will take a long time to blow up and if it is too small, it will not hold much air. Also, it is wise to have multiple balloons (just in case there is difficulty with the first balloon). Buy balloons that are easy to blow up.

Beads: During this series, the group members will be making a bead wristband that, when completed, will tell their stories. The teens will fill out a journal sheet with information about a topic and select beads that depict different things on the journal sheet. Usually the colors of the beads that they pick are symbolic of something they have talked about in the session and written about on their journal sheets. They are shown the beads during the journal activity, but they do not actually pick them out or string them until week 9. Then, they spend the whole journal time in week 9 beading their wristbands. When the wristbands are completed, each teen can tell his or her story using the wristband. Buy a variety of bead colors for them to choose for their bead wristbands. Use either elastic bands and no clasps or fishing line with clasps.

Bio-Dots®: Bio-dots® are used to show the group members the connection between the mind and the body. The Bio-dot® is a small dot that is placed on the flesh part between the thumb and forefinger on the back of the hand. The idea is that the Bio-dot® changes colors depending on how much stress we feel. Group members are led through a series of relaxation and breathing exercises and asked to check their Bio-dots® to see if they changed color as a result of these exercises. Order the dots and cards from: BioDot International, Inc. P.O. Box 2246 Indianapolis, Indiana, 46206. Phone: 1 (800) 272-2340 or (312) 537-5776. Price: $10.00 per 100 or $66.00 per 1000 plus $1.50 postage and handling. Each order contains an instruction guide, a small poster, and 10 color codes (cards).

Bio-Dot® Cards: These are color codes that explain what the colors on the Bio-dot® mean and can be ordered with the Bio-dots® (see above).

Blank Paper: Blank paper is used throughout the curricula for various activities. One week, it is used for the teens to draw "sad." Another week, blank paper is used for writing affirmation notes to other group members. Here, each group member and the facilitator writes their names at the bottom of their sheet. Then the sheet is passed to the person to their left. Then that person writes a note of encouragement or affirmation to the person whose name appears at the bottom of the sheet. Once they have written their note to that person, they fold the paper over to cover their message and pass it to the person to their left. Keep going until everyone has written a note to everyone else. Blank paper is also used when the teens write letters to new group members. They can pass on letters of encouragement and things they learned. 8½" × 11" blank paper is appropriate for all activities. In case the teens want to draw pictures of themselves, use neutral colored paper tones, such as blue, violet, green, or goldenrod, that do not resemble skin tones so that teens of color do not have to draw themselves as white. Or, purchase multi-cultural crayons (see Crayons below).

Bowl (to burn post-its in): At the end of the coulda-woulda-shoulda activity (see below) the teens are asked to think about which coulda-woulda-shouldas they might be open to let go of and what ones they need to hold onto for now. Now they are asked to tear up the ones they want to let go of and put them into a bowl where they are mixed up. Burn the torn pieces of paper as a symbol of letting go. Put a small candle (perhaps a tea light) in a bowl and then add the post-its to be burned. A large ceramic or metal bowl can be used. Then the group should decide as a whole what to do with the ashes. Should they be strewn in the soil to feed a plant, flower, or tree? In this way the group has, as a whole, taken something negative and turned it into a positive

Bubble Wrap: Give the teens a square of bubble wrap to pop for one of their breaks. They really get into the sound and action of popping the bubbles.

Camera with Film: A group picture is taken the second to last (9th) session. At the conclusion of week 10 each group member will be given a copy of the picture. Be sure to take a couple of pictures to insure a good shot.

Candle, Matches: One or more candles might be used during the group sessions. Candles add light to the room, especially if there isn't bright overhead lighting. They also add warmth to the room. In particular, a candle is used as a focal point during the centering and closing exercises. It's best to buy candles that are in a metal or glass container to reduce the risk of fire. It is important to be very careful when using candles as the wax or flame can cause injuries. Please take every precaution to avoid any problems.

Cassette or CD Player, Soft Music: A cassette or CD player is used with soft music while the teens are doing journal writing each week.

Centering Activity Overview: This is a script for guiding the teens in a "centering" which is often used to begin the sessions. This script for leading the centering activity can be found in Appendix 2.

Centering Candle: See Candle (above).

Change Cards: Change cards describe various changes that can take place when a special person dies. Each change card should be copied onto colored card stock paper, then laminated or covered with clear contact paper. The teens take turns picking the change cards, and respond whether they have or have not experienced that change since the death of their special person. Change cards can be found in Appendix 2.

Check-in Sheet: Try to vary the ways the teens check in each week. One way is to use the check-in sheet. Teens are asked to make a mark on the check-in sheet from 1–10. 1 = the pits! 5 = so-so, and 10 = great. This is a visual way to see where the teen sees him- or herself. It also invites them to talk about what made them put themselves on the scale in this way. The check-in sheet can be found in Appendix 2.

Childhood Depression Inventory (CDI): Group members are administered a brief (27 item) depression inventory (Kovacs, 1992) both at the start and the end of the curriculum. The CDI can be obtained by contacting Multi-Health Systems, Inc. 908 Niagara Falls Blvd., North Tonawanda, NY, 14120-2060. Fax: 1-416-424-1736 or Phone: 1-416-424-1700.

Code of Safety: In the second session, the teens come up with rules so that they can all feel safe in the group. The rules are written, by the facilitator, on a piece of tagboard. Tagboard is used because it is sturdier than a piece of colored paper or copy paper. A piece about 11″ × 17″ should be sufficient size.

Colored Die: The colored die is used in conjunction with the grief reaction cards (described below). Use a small wooden block and cut out colored circles matching the colors of the grief reaction cards that have been copied onto neon colored card stock paper. Then cover each circle with clear contact paper. During the grief reaction card exercise the teens throw the die and pick a card that corresponds to the color on the die.

Common Grief Reactions Checklist (CGRC): The CGRC (Jimerson, 1997) contains 65 common grief reactions of children and teens. It is administered both at the beginning and the end of the curriculum. The CGRC can be found in Appendix 2.

Coulda-woulda-shoulda Post-its: These post-its are used in conjunction with the activity that explores any residual regret or guilt that the teens may have around the death. Buy the smallest size post-its and write "coulda" on one, "shoulda" on another, and "woulda" on the last. Make sure that each teen gets a set. The teens are then asked to place each post-it on themselves as a way of signifying how guilt can stick to them. They then discuss which ones they can let go of, and remove them, symbolically letting go of this guilt.

Crayons: Crayons are used frequently in the groups. They are much easier to use if they are put into plastic containers with covers rather than the boxes that the crayons come in. Having the crayons accessible in big containers allows the teens to use them easily and relieves the hassle of getting the right crayons into the right box. Crayola® now offers multicultural crayons with various skin tone shades. These are ideal, so that teens of color can draw themselves. If multicultural crayons are not available, have the teens draw on colored sheets of paper, such as blue or green, which neutralize the drawing surface (see Blank Paper above) so that teens of color don't have to draw themselves as white.

Death Art: During the session on exploring death, as an optional activity, the teens are shown some art that illustrates how death has been depicted by artists through the ages. As teens look at the pictures, the facilitator might ask questions such as, "What are the artists saying about death in the pictures?" and "How do you feel when you look at the pictures?" At the local library, go to the Art Resource Room (if there is one) and ask to look at and check out some of the files they have on death. Alternately use art books with paintings or drawings that depict death. When choosing pictures, try to pick pictures that are artist's depictions of death.

Directions for Relaxation and Breathing Exercises: During the self-care session, the teens are taught breathing and relaxation exercises. They are also used in conjunction with the Bio-dots® so that the teens can see how such exercises change their bodies. The directions can be found in Appendix 2.

Drawing Sheets: During several sessions, teens do a drawing activity where they are given a sheet of paper that has a topic listed at the top. Sometimes this is done instead of journal writing, other times it is done in addition, and other times it is offered as an optional activity. Completed drawing sheets are put into the teen's folders. All drawing sheets can be found in Appendix 2.

"Me Before/After the Death": This drawing sheet asks teens to draw a picture of themselves before the death and after the death. It is intended to reinforce that the death of a special person changes us on a personal level. If teens do not want to draw themselves, ask them to draw themselves as a tree or animal. What kind of tree or animal were they before the death? What kind of tree or animal are they now? Are the the same tree or animal? If so, how have they changed? Then have them draw that. After they have drawn their pictures have them talk about the pictures they have drawn. If they do not want to show their pictures to others in the group, have them talk about what they drew.

"My Best Memory": Teens are asked to draw a picture of their best memory with their special person. If they have difficulty thinking of just one best memory, have them choose just one favorite memory.

"My Last Memory": Teens are asked to draw the last memory they have of their special person. In other words, they draw the last time they spent with their special person before he or she died. The exception to this exercise would be if the death was traumatic and the teen witnessed the death. In this instance, the potential for retraumatization is high and must be assessed before this exercise is done. If a teen witnessed a traumatic death, you may want them to draw a picture of the last time they spent time with the special person before the death.

"Something That Makes Me Mad, Sad, Scared, and Happy": During the week that the teens talk about identifying and expressing feelings, they are asked to identify something that makes them or has made them mad, sad, scared, and happy since the death of their special person and to depict each of these in a drawing.

"This is what death looks like to me": After looking at the way artists have depicted death through the ages (see Death Art above), teens draw their own interpretation of what death looks like.

"This is what I remember about the funeral" or **"This is what I remember about the day my special person died":** Both of these sheets invite the teen to draw either what he or she remembers about the funeral or about the day his or her special person died.

Elastic (or fishing wire and clasps): During week 9, the teens make their beaded wristbands. They will string the beads that they have been choosing each week. Use elastic and help the teens tie it, or fishing wire with clasps. See beads (above).

Feeling Circle: The feeling circle is another variation for a check-in. Teens are asked to think about how they are feeling right at that moment. Teens are asked to divide up the circle into parts reflecting their feelings. For example, if the teen is feeling very sad and a little confused, he or she will divide the circle into two parts, with the biggest part depicting sad and the smaller part depicting confused. They can be encouraged to choose different colors to represent different feelings, or use shapes to depict the feelings. Once they have completed their circles, have them talk about what they drew as a way to check-in. The feeling circle can be found in Appendix 2.

Feeling Faces Sheet: For check-in during a few sessions, use a sheet that has drawings of faces with various expressions, depicting common feelings. Teens are asked to circle the feeling(s) that best depict how they are feeling. Then they use this sheet during check-in to talk about how they are feeling. It is important to copy this sheet onto colored paper that does not represent a skin tone. For more explanation, see Blank Paper (above). The feeling faces sheet can be found in Appendix 2.

Feeling Sentence Starters: These cards have incomplete sentences on them. Teens take turns choosing a card and completing the sentence on the card. All of the phrases have to do with feelings and how teens may express them. Feeling sentence starters can be found in Appendix 2.

Feelings of Grief List: This list is provided for the teens as they work on journal sheet #4, to give them ideas for 'feeling' words. The feelings of grief list can be found in Appendix 2.

Fight and Flight Cards: These cards have phrases on them that describe two different ways of coping with grief that do not allow people to feel the pain of their loss. The first coping mechanism is to "fight"—to keep moving, talking, staying busy, etc. The second is "flight"—to ignore or minimize the pain of grief. Teens are asked to select a card from the fight pile and the flight pile. They are asked to respond to each card by saying whether they have responded to their grief in either of the two ways. If they have, they keep the cards. If they have not, they discard the card. At the completion of the exercise, the group members can then see in which way they respond more often or if they use the defenses equally. This exercise is intended to educate teens about the ways in which they respond to grief. These cards can be found in Appendix 2.

Folders: Use pocket folders to hold all paper materials that are created or used by the teens during the 10 sessions, including handouts, drawings, check-in sheets, and journal sheets. At the end of the curriculum, this makes up the teen's "journal." The folders should be kept by the facilitator until the end of the curriculum. Do not let the teens take them home until the completion of the series. Buy pocket folders that have three prongs in them so that the teens can put their journal sheets in the folders in this way. Punch three holes in all sheets so that they can easily fit in the folders. Individual activities do not list folders as a material, however, it is assumed that the teens will have them each week so that they can put papers in them as needed. These folders are also referred to as the teen's "journals." (See Journals below).

Funeral Photos: These are pictures of things and places commonly associated with the death or the funeral. These photos include photos of caskets, a funeral home, an altar, a cemetery, a church, a hospital, and an urn for cremation ashes. These photos can be found in Appendix 2.

Games: Each session, provide some developmentally appropriate games, such as puzzles, books, and cards to be used by teens who arrive early.

Grief Reaction Cards: The grief reaction cards have common grief reactions of teens written on them. Copy them onto neon colored card stock paper. Each category of reactions is copied onto a different color. The reaction categories are physical, mental, social, emotional, and warning signs. This activity is intended to normalize reactions teens may be experiencing since the death. Teens are asked to throw the die and choose the grief reaction card that matches the colored circle on the die. Then they are asked to respond to whether they have experienced this reaction since the death. Keep going until all of the cards have been picked. Ask others to respond to each card as well and then keep track of their responses. At the conclusion of the activity, report to them which responses they all endorsed the most. The grief reaction cards can be found in Appendix 2.

Grief Support Groups General Information Sheet (GIS): The GIS (Jimerson, 1997) is a list of questions to be used by the facilitator as a semistructured interview during the week 1 information interviews. It provides the facilitators with some information about the teen before the group begins, including information about the teen's school, relationships, his or her relationship to the deceased, etc. A GIS is filled out for each individual teen. A copy of the questions are included in the text of the Week 1 session, and an additional GIS, for photocopying, is included in Appendix 2.

Group Evaluations: This evaluation sheet is used for the teens to evaluate their experience in the group. When teens fill out the sheet leave the room or go to another part of the room so that teens feel comfortable saying what they need to say on the evaluation. Ask for a volunteer to put the evaluations in an envelope and give them to your program director. The group evaluation form can be found in Appendix 2.

Group Pictures: A group picture is taken in Week 9. Each group member is given a copy of the picture at the conclusion of session 10 to reinforce to each other that they can continue to be sources of support to each other as the group nears an end. It is important to obtain permission to take a picture of each teen from each caregiver; and this is included as part of the GIS to be completed with the caregiver in week 1 (See Camera with Film above).

Handout, "Grief Keys": Grief Keys is a handout that is used each week as the session topic is introduced. Grief Keys are used to help the teens with their grief as they move through life and experience different kinds of losses. If those losses are put away and never grieved, the thoughts, feelings, and reactions around each of these losses never get expressed and then go into the next loss. Then when the teen grieves that loss, the grief is bigger than it needs to be. Grief Keys help in two ways: first they help to keep the feelings about loss unlocked so that it is possible to stay in touch with our grief; second, grief keys are all of the things that can be done to help with grief. The questions in the middle are questions that need answers when there is a loss. The suggestions on the right are things to do to help with grief. Each one of the Grief Keys will be addressed in one of the sessions in the series. Note that they are not addressed in order (i.e. key 1 is addressed first, key 3 is addressed second, etc.) The handout helps to frame for the teens the kinds of things that will be addressed throughout the course of the series. The Grief Keys Handout can be found in Appendix 2.

Journal Sheets: Toward the end of almost every session, teens are given an opportunity to do some journal writing or drawing. Leave about 15–20 minutes of the session for this activity. Put on a CD or cassette tape with soft instrumental music to encourage the teens to get into a reflective mode. Teens should be encouraged to spread out throughout the room in order to be alone with their thoughts.

Go over the journal sheets with the teens before they begin so that they understand them. Completed journal sheets go in the teens's folders, which at the end of the curriculum will make up their "journals."

On the journal sheets, teens are asked to pick certain colors of beads that represent things that they are writing about. Teens will refer back to these portions of the journal sheets during week 9 when they bead their wristbands. See beads (above). Journal sheets can be found in Appendix 2.

Journal Sheet #1: This first journal entry asks the teens to describe themselves in words and in colors before and after the death. This sheet is used in conjunction with the adjective list (above).

Journal Sheet #2: This journal sheet addresses the changes the teen has experienced since the death, including family or friend changes and personal changes.

Journal Sheet #3: This journal sheet has teens reflect on their relationship with their special person and think about a special memory they have of him or her.

Journal Sheet #4: This journal sheet asks the teens to reflect on the different feelings they have experienced since the death and how they express them.

Journal Sheet #5: This journal sheet has teens reflect on healthy ways to cope with their feelings and on their group experience.

Journal: The folders (see above) are also referred to as "journals." By week 9, the teens's folders will be filled with journal sheets and drawings that they have compiled through the sessions (see Journal Sheets and Drawing Sheets above). The full journals will be referred to in week 9, as the teens bead their wristbands (see beads above). See Folders (above) for further description of the types of folders used for the journals.

Koosh® Ball: Koosh® balls are soft plastic balls of long stringy spines. It is used to help the teens tell their stories for the first time to the group. The facilitator throws the Koosh® ball to a teen who must answer a question from a story card (described below). That teen then throws the ball to another teen and asks him or her a question from a story card. The process is repeated until all of the cards are gone.

Love Notes: Love notes are used at the conclusion of the session on unfinished business. Teens are asked to write their special person a love note, saying all of the things that they didn't get to say or would like to say to them. They can also draw pictures on it. These are half-sheets of paper decorated with a border and called 'Love Notes.' Since the teens will take the notes with them, spend some time helping the teens think about what they will do with the notes. Perhaps they would like to take them to the cemetery or put them in a special place. Notes are sent home to the caregivers explaining what these love notes are and how they can help their teens decide what to do with the notes (notes to caregivers can be found in Appendix 3). 'Love notes' can be found in Appendix 2.

Mad Target & Wet Sponges: The mad target is a bulls-eye style target (as used for archery) at which the wet sponges will be thrown. This bulls-eye target may be made by drawing on a shower curtain using permanent markers (usually the inside circle is colored red). It is also possible to purchase prefabricated targets at sporting good stores and archery shops. If targets are purchased it is best to select water-proof versions or to laminate paper versions so they will be reuseable. If this activity is done inside, it is best to use a plastic sheet or a shower curtain on the floor to collect water. To limit the amount of water in each sponge cut the sponges into smaller pieces (heavy enough to throw when soaked with water, but not so large as to drench an entire wall). Don't forget a few towels to soak up the water from the shower curtain. This activity is an example of a healthy way to get out mad feelings.

Markers: Markers should be a staple in the group's supplies. Refrain from letting teens draw with them since they don't afford much opportunity for artistic expression. No matter how hard they press the markers on a drawing sheet, it always looks the same. Crayons, on the other hand, can show a wider range of expression depending on how hard you press the crayons on the sheet of paper. Markers can be used for making signs, writing the Code of Safety, or for group members to use to decorate their puzzle pieces.

Matches: See Candles (above).

Memory Cards: Memory cards have various memories written on them that the teens are asked to remember when they play the memory game. Copy the memory cards onto brightly colored card stock paper and cover with clear contact paper. Memory cards can be found in Appendix 2.

Name Tags: Put name tags on the teens for the first few weeks. Facilitators also wear name tags. Be certain to spell each teen's name correctly and use the name he or she prefers. Sometimes, it is fun to allow teens to draw or color on their name tags after their name has been written on it. Because the groups are limited in size, the teens and facilitators usually learn each other's name after the first couple of weeks. Purchase name tags for teens in an office supply or craft store, or make them.

Pencils: Pencils should be a staple in the group's supplies. Use #2 pencils with erasers. Pencils are primarily used when the teens do worksheets or check-in, however, and are not used for drawings. Remove pencils prior to a drawing exercise, as crayons are much more expressive.

Pictures/Belongings of Special People: During the session on memories/remembering, teens share with other group members pictures they brought and/or other personal belongings that remind them of their special person. Teens can pass around the things that they have brought if they want, but they don't have to.

Plastic Sheet: See Mad Targets & Wet Sponges (above).

Play-doh®: Have an ample supply of Play-doh® for the groups. It should be a staple in the group's materials. Play-doh® is used in several sessions. Teens use it to sculpt "sad" in one session. In the "Identifying Changes" session, the teens are encouraged to "change" the Play-doh® as they discuss changes. This gives the teens a chance to relax and also provides the facilitators with an opportunity to watch the teens as they engage in these activities. These activities may yield additional information about what the teen is thinking.

Prescriptions for Feelings: Prescriptions are included for sad, scared, and mad feelings. Each is a small piece of paper containing healthy ways to deal with each of these feelings (e.g., breathe deeply, etc.). These prescriptions are provided for discussion during the group; then each group participant may take their prescriptions home with them. Examples of prescriptions can be found in Appendix 2.

Problem Solving Plan Handout: This handout is used to help group members learn how to solve the problems that confront them. Teens are asked to think of a problem that they are dealing with right now, and they are asked to use the plan to help them solve it. If they cannot think of any problems, use the problem solving scenarios provided (see below). This handout can be found in Appendix 2.

Problem Solving Scenarios: The problem solving scenarios sheet lists several possible problems that teens this age might encounter. Facilitator may use these if the teens cannot come up with problems that they are personally experiencing. It is used in conjunction with the problem solving plan handout (see above). The problem solving scenarios can be found in Appendix 2.

Puzzle Pieces: The puzzle pieces are used as a technique to help group members connect with each other right from the start. Take a large piece of tagboard and draw a heart on it. Draw the heart in such a way as it takes up most of the piece of tagboard. Now, cut the tagboard up into enough pieces so that everyone in the group, including facilitators gets a piece. Now the teens are asked to draw personal things about themselves on their own puzzle piece. Once the teens have gotten to know each other better through this activity, they put the puzzle together with each other's help. By working together during the very first session, it is hoped that the group members learn that they need to depend on each other and help each other out when they are in a group. The puzzle pieces are brought out and discussed again during the final session. As they leave the group they take the puzzle pieces with them. The puzzle piece reminds them that they are not alone. The puzzle pieces (template) can be found in Appendix 2.

Relaxation Activity: This is used as an alternative script for the centering activity overview during the session that focuses on coping with feelings. It teaches the teens how to relax themselves and then take themselves on an imaginary journey. These are techniques they can use at various times; for example, if they cannot fall or stay asleep at night. The relaxation activity can be found in Appendix 2.

Resource List: Give teens a resource list at the first full session (Week 2). This resource list includes crisis intervention line phone numbers and other resources available to teens in your local community. Include the hours that these resources are available (i.e., 9 a.m. to 5 p.m., 24 hours a day, etc.). Teens take this list home with them. A sample resource list can be found in Appendix 2.

Sample Notes to be Sent Home to Caregivers: Each week a note is sent home to the caregivers. The notes let the caregivers know what the teens did in group. They include reminders, when applicable, to have the teen bring something the following week. For example, the note for Week 3 reminds them that the teens are to bring a picture of their special person, as well as any object that reminds the teens of their special person, with them the following week. Sample notes can be found in Appendix 3.

Snacks: Facilitators may decide if they wish to provide snacks each week, or just for the party on the final session. Whenever snacks are offered, be careful to check out possible food allergies with caregivers. Try to offer healthy snacks like fruit-filled breakfast bars or crackers. Individual juice drinks are handy to use for beverages. If snacks are offered each week, plan discussions around snack time.

Story Cards: Story Cards are used as a way for the teens to tell their stories for the first time to the group. Teens take turns throwing a Koosh® ball (described above) and whoever catches it is asked a question from a story card by the teen who threw it. The teen is given an opportunity to discard up to two cards, if he or she doesn't want to answer the question that was posed. In this way, the teens learn that they are very much in charge of their own stories. Story Cards can be found in Appendix 2.

Support Wheel: The support wheel helps group members to see the amount and kind of support they have in their lives. Each of the spokes on the wheel represents a different kind of support. Teens are asked to think of someone in their lives that can offer them each of the kinds of support on the spokes of the wheel. The concept of a support wheel is used to illustrate what can happen if there isn't enough support in a teen's life. Just as a wheel may break down or not be able to roll smoothly with missing spokes, so it is with humans. Show the teens that they cannot move through their grief with missing spokes. The support wheel can be found in Appendix 2.

Tagboard: See Code of Safety (above).

Tea Lights: Tea lights are used for the closing ceremony at the end of the memories/remembering session. Each teen is given a tea light and he or she goes to the center, shares a memory of his or her special person, and lights the candle (from the main taper candle) in memory of the special person. Teens take their tea lights home. It is important to emphasize that the teens can only have their candles lit when they are around an adult; since the candles are sent home, they should be accompanied by a note to the caregivers.

Thought Stopping Worksheet: This worksheet is used to teach the teens the concept of thought stopping. Thought stopping is a technique to stop a negative thought and replace it with a more positive thought. This technique is especially effective when thoughts are obsessive. Teens are given an example on the worksheet of such thoughts in regard to mad, sad, and scared feelings. They are asked then to replace them with new thoughts. Thought stopping is taught to help them cope with their feelings. The thought stopping worksheet can be found in Appendix 2.

Wet Sponges: See Mad Target & Wet Sponges (above).

"What I Think About Death" Cards: Each card contains a statement that reflects a common attitude/belief about death (i.e., "all things happen for a reason, even bad things"). Teens take turns responding to the statements on the cards. This exercise is done to explore one's personal beliefs and attitudes and to talk about them in a safe setting. These cards can be found in Appendix 2.

Samples of Materials to be Used

ADJECTIVE LIST

SOME EXAMPLES OF WORDS

Brave	Cute	Confident
Intelligent	Talented	Dramatic
Energetic	Artistic	Quick
Pretty	Musical	Friendly
Strong	Creative	Helpful
Courageous	Logical	Truthful
Humorous	Wise	Likable
Serious	Inventive	Ambitious
Playful	Talkative	Mature
Kind	Thoughtful	Curious
Sensitive	Dependable	
Quiet	Honest	

AFFIRMATIONS

Even though my special person had died, I know that not all of my life will be painful.

My opinions are important.

I have the right to be heard.

I deserve attention.

I can do the right thing.

I don't have to do everything myself.

My ideas are valuable.

It's OK to make mistakes.

My dreams are my own.

People can say what they want about me. I know I'm cool.

It's OK to be silly.

I have no need to be the center of attention all of the time.

Everyone has something that they're good at.

I can learn to do anything if I practice and have the right teacher.

I have something important to say.

All problems have solutions. If I cannot solve a problem, I need to ask for help.

It's OK to disagree with someone.

People can have differences and still be friends.

It's OK to be angry or feel hurt, but it helps to talk to someone about it.

I have never done anything so bad that I can't talk about it with someone I trust.

I can learn from my mistakes.

I will be good to myself.

AFFIRMATIONS

It's OK to lose.

It's OK to fail.

Problems are situations I can learn from.

If I don't understand something about my situation, I can ask questions.

I trust myself.

I may not be able to trust everyone, but I can trust some people.

I need to let people take care of me.

I try to do the right thing.

I can make good choices.

I can find healthy ways to express my feelings.

I don't need to hurt myself or anyone else.

I believe in myself.

I am growing more beautiful everyday.

I am not alone.

I am a survivor.

I am smart.

I can learn anything I want to learn.

I am generous.

I am wise.

I like who I am becoming.

I will allow myself to change.

My opinions are important.

AFFIRMATIONS

It's OK to be angry.

It's OK to be sad.

I can be fearful and courageous at the same time.

I have the power to change myself. It takes courage to walk away from a fight.

It takes courage to say, "I'm sorry."

All I have to do is be myself.

Going at my own pace is the way for me to make progress.

All that is required of me is to do my best.

I don't have to compare myself to anyone else.

I will be gentle with myself.

I will give myself a break because I am doing the best that I can.

No one has the right to push me around or to hurt me.

I don't have to listen to someone who is putting me down.

I'm worth standing up for.

I don't have to fix anything or anyone. I can accept them for who they are.

I have the power to succeed.

I don't have to give my power away by letting others get to me or make me angry.

Asking questions, even ones I think are dumb, is OK.

I am acting my age.

I am a lovable person.

I am stronger than I think.

I will be happy again.

AFFIRMATIONS

I know I can ask for help when I don't know how to solve a problem.

I know that there are some things in my life I cannot change, I can only change the way I handle them.

I am a feeling person. It is OK to feel my feelings.

I know that I did not cause the death.

I know that I can communicate with my special person whenever I want to.

I can handle the stress of my grief better when I take care of my body.

I promise to myself that I will talk about my loss with someone I trust.

I know that I am not responsible for other people's feelings.

I know that I have worth.

I am open to receiving help from others.

I will not let others make me angry.

I know that it's OK to have fun once in a while even though my special person has died.

I must trust that I am safe.

In order to get help for myself, I must ask for it.

I can share my story with others I can trust, so that they can understand me better.

I can recall memories of my special person and share them with others.

I can pay attention to my behavior. It will tell me when I need to get my feelings out.

My grief is unique as every snowflake. I will let myself grieve in my own way.

When my grief comes out sideways, I will pay attention to it.

Other people might tell me how I should feel, but I will feel what I need to feel.

Even when I don't want to share my grief with anyone, I will find someone who will listen to my pain.

AFFIRMATIONS

Every day I will check in with my feelings.

Sometimes I don't take care of myself. I know that in order to take care of my grief, I must take care of myself.

I know that sometimes I cannot show other people how I feel. But at the end of the day I need to take a look at that moment again.

I am a human being. I am a thinking being. I am also a feeling being. I can let myself feel. It is an important part of me.

No question is a dumb question. If I have questions, I can ask them.

I don't always have to talk about how I feel; I can also draw my feelings or write about them.

Even though I don't want to face my grief at times, I know that to face it, is the only way to heal.

I know that if I do not let myself grieve, it will go underground until I am ready to face it.

I will not always be this sad.

I will feel good about having fun again someday.

I need to take breaks from my grief sometimes, and let myself have fun.

Sometimes life may not feel safe enough for me to grieve. I will find a space where I feel safe so that I can allow myself to grieve.

Grief is like walking in deep snow. I may not feel like I am getting anywhere and it's hard work . . . But if I take my grief one step at a time, I can heal.

I know that everyone in my family may be in a different place with their grief. I will respect where each person is and not compare myself to them.

Just like tapestry material that looks ugly and frazzled on one side, my grief can be woven into the fabric of my life and on the other side can become a part of a life that is beautiful.

I know that I can talk to my special person anytime I want to.

AFFIRMATIONS

It's OK for me to feel mad that my special person died, as long as I don't hurt anyone or anything else.

I need to let myself become friends with other people who have had a special person die. I know that they understand and we can help each other out.

I need to let other people love me.

Sometimes it's not safe to share my grief with some people. I need to figure out whom I am safe with.

It is not my fault that my special person died.

Grief can be a lonely experience. I know that I am not alone.

If something bothers me about death, I need to tell someone about it.

I can write notes to my special person and put them in a special place.

Just because my special person has died, does not mean that this is the end of my story. There will be many more chapters in my life.

Sometimes a rainbow appears at the end of a storm . . . I will trust that there will be rainbows at the end of my grief.

I will grieve my special person on and off as I grow up.

When people have been mean to me, I can take a bath or shower and wash their meanness off of me.

I don't have to prove how tough I am to anyone. It's enough to know that I am tough on the inside.

Sometimes when I am alone at night, I get scared or sad. I need to tell myself that I will be OK.

Even though my life is very sad right now, I know that I will be happy again someday.

I will remember my special person always.

I will talk about my special person so that other people won't forget him/her.

AFFIRMATIONS

No one can replace my special person, but I can let other people into my life that care about me.

Sometimes help comes from places I don't expect. I will be open to the possibility that help can come in different ways.

Sometimes my grief makes it hard for me to sleep. I need to watch sodas and other drinks that have caffeine in them. These drinks will keep me awake. It would be better to drink water or caffeine-free drinks after supper.

Exercise will help to take away the rough edges of my grief. I will try to exercise several times each week.

When I get too tired, my grief is harder to deal with. I need to make sure that I get enough sleep.

Elephants are one of the few types of animals who openly grieve the death of a special person. I will let elephants remind me that it is OK to grieve. It's OK to grieve.

I know that if I ignore my grief, it won't go anywhere, it will be waiting for me when I want to take a look at it.

It takes a lot of courage to grieve. I will grieve with courage.

I can imagine myself in an invisible bubble. I can keep some people from entering my bubble and hurting me. I can let other people into my bubble. I feel safe in my bubble.

Even though my grief can feel cold and harsh, I can trust in the promis of spring and know that I will not always feel the same.

Tomorrow I promise to share my feelings with someone.

I need to find people who can tell me about my special person. Things that maybe I don't know. I will find someone who can tell me a story about my special person.

CENTERING ACTIVITY OVERVIEW

Tonight we are going to take some time to do a centering. Centering means that we are going to take a trip in our imaginations. I want everyone to find a place on the floor where they can lie down. Make sure that you aren't touching anyone else. It's really important that everyone be very quiet. Instead of talking during our centering, I want you to remember the things you want to share or the answers to the questions, and we will talk about them at the end. Even if you are having a hard time imagining the trip, you still need to be very quiet and still so everyone else can do it. Okay, let's see who can be the quietest.

Close your eyes and take a quiet, deep breath in. And let it out. Breathe in. And out. Good. Now I want you to imagine a warm, soft, fluffy cloud floating gently down to you. You climb on top of the cloud and it curls up around you, so you can't fall off. Now it lifts up from the floor and it flies out the door and down the hall and outside. You can see the trees and building getting smaller and smaller as you float higher in the sky. Maybe you see a bird or two. Or maybe you see an airplane. What things can you see in the sky that you can remember to share with us later? You can smell the fresh air, and you feel very safe and peaceful on your cloud. Now it's time to turn around and to fly back to group. What sounds do you hear as you are flying? Now you can see the building and your car in the parking lot. Now you are flying lower. You fly in the door and down the hall and into the room and your cloud sets you down very gently on the floor. You know that whenever you want to feel safe and peaceful, you can call your cloud and it will float down for you. Take one last deep breath. Breathe in. And out. Whenever you are ready, you can open your eyes.

The facilitator then talks with the teens about how it felt to fly on a cloud. What sorts of things did they see or hear? Where would they like to fly on their clouds next time?

CHANGE CARDS

Special person doesn't eat with me anymore	I eat less food
We eat different food now	No one talks at the table
There is an empty chair at the table now	We don't sit at the table anymore
I don't get tucked in anymore	I can't get to sleep

CHANGE CARDS

I am scared of the dark now	I sleep somewhere else now
I have nightmares now	I don't get hugged anymore
My family doesn't have fun anymore	I watch more TV
People fight more	No one talks to each other anymore

CHANGE CARDS

I don't get to see the person who died anymore	Sometimes I wet my pants
Someone else bathes me	My family doesn't play outside anymore
We stay home more	I have to go to a sitter now

CHECK–IN SHEET

NAME _____

DATE _____

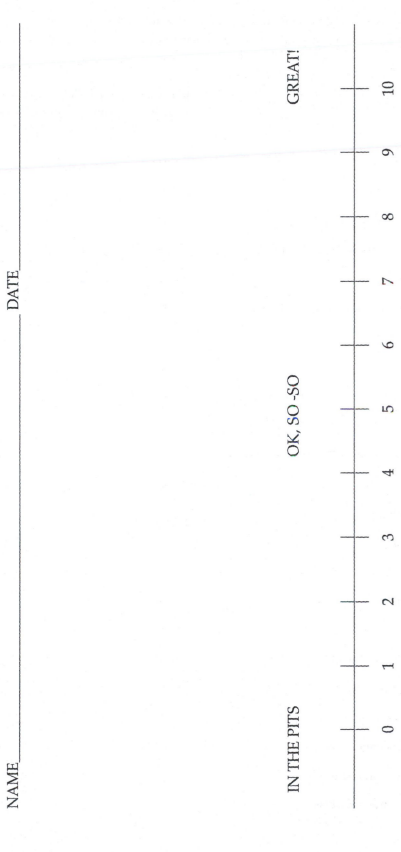

IN THE PITS   OK, SO -SO   GREAT!

0   1   2   3   4   5   6   7   8   9   10

COMMON GRIEF REACTIONS CHECKLIST (CGRC)

The following list contains common grief reactions in children and teens.
Please fill the circle indicating the degree to which the child has experienced each item since the loss.

	not at all/ none	a little/ sometimes	a lot/ often	currently a problem
Loss of appetite	○	○	○	○
Increased appetite	○	○	○	○
Difficulty falling asleep	○	○	○	○
Nightmares and/or night terrors	○	○	○	○
Bedwetting	○	○	○	○
Reappearnce of toileting accidents	○	○	○	○
Stomachaches	○	○	○	○
Headaches	○	○	○	○
Frequent colds or other physical illness	○	○	○	○
Fatigue	○	○	○	○
Appears uninterested in typical activities	○	○	○	○
Irritability	○	○	○	○
Guilty feelings	○	○	○	○
Mood swings	○	○	○	○
Suicidal thoughts/behaviors	○	○	○	○
Panic attacks	○	○	○	○
Marked improvement in behavior	○	○	○	○
Marked worsening of behavior	○	○	○	○
Increase in activity	○	○	○	○
Decrease in activity	○	○	○	○
Often thinks about the loss	○	○	○	○
Shorter attention span	○	○	○	○
Short term memory loss	○	○	○	○

COMMON GRIEF REACTIONS CHECKLIST (CGRC)

	not at all/ none	a little/ sometimes	a lot/ often	currently a problem
Difficulty concentrating	o	o	o	o
Often distracted	o	o	o	o
Seems afraid to separate from caregiver(s)	o	o	o	o
Seems more anxious	o	o	o	o
Withdraws from friends and family	o	o	o	o
Displays immature behaviors	o	o	o	o
Aggressive toward others	o	o	o	o
Behaves destructively	o	o	o	o
Behaves compulsively	o	o	o	o
Steals	o	o	o	o
Increase in independence	o	o	o	o
Increase in dependency	o	o	o	o
Increase in caregiving behaviors	o	o	o	o
Increase in pleasing behaviors	o	o	o	o
Depressed	o	o	o	o
Hyperactive (excessive activity)	o	o	o	o
Abuses alcohol/drugs	o	o	o	o
School grades have improved	o	o	o	o
School behavior has improved	o	o	o	o
School grades have dropped	o	o	o	o
Behavior problems at school	o	o	o	o
Is concerned about own or other's safety	o	o	o	o
Reenacts the traumatic event	o	o	o	o
Difficulty staying awake	o	o	o	o
Seems more impulsive	o	o	o	o
Pessimistic expectations of future	o	o	o	o

COMMON GRIEF REACTIONS CHECKLIST (CGRC)

	not at all/ none	a little/ sometimes	a lot/ often	currently a problem
Fears being ostracized by peers	o	o	o	o
Forsees a shortened future	o	o	o	o
Has flashbacks or re-experiences the event	o	o	o	o
Experiences nausea	o	o	o	o
Avoids reminders of the event	o	o	o	o
Diarrhea	o	o	o	o
Trouble breathing	o	o	o	o
Is unable to remember parts of the event	o	o	o	o
Cries easily	o	o	o	o
Behaviorally imitates the deceased	o	o	o	o
Startles easily	o	o	o	o
Trembles or shakes	o	o	o	o
Is eating too much	o	o	o	o
Is not eating enough	o	o	o	o
Takes more risks (Please Specify)	o	o	o	o

_____

_____

_____

Please note any additional reactions the child has had since the loss:

_____

_____

_____

_____

_____

DIRECTIONS FOR RELAXATION AND BREATHING EXERCISES

Facilitator asks the teens to pretend that there is large balloon in their stomach. Facilitator tells them to listen as he/she counts "1–2–3–4." They fill up their stomachs with air. Teens inhale 1–2–3–4. Facilitator has them HOLD in the air. Then, "let all of the air out of the balloon." Teens exhale.

Facilitator says,
"Curl your toes up in your shoes, then let them relax.
Now let your toes relax inside your shoe.
Now press your feet into the floor as hard as you can.
Now let your feet rest comfortably on the floor.
Tighten the muscles in your arm as hard as you can, now let them relax.
Tighten the muscles in your neck and shrug your shoulders up as high as you can.
Now relax the muscles in your neck and shoulders.
Now make a frown with your face as tight as you can.
Now relax all of the muscles in your face.
Now pretend that a giant wave of relaxation is moving up your body from your toes all the way up your body to the top of your head. Imagine that all of the tension is going out the top of your head.
Now look at your Bio-dot®. Did it change colors?"

Facilitator reviews what is on the back of the card with the teens and encourages them to use it whenever they want. "One way we can take care of ourselves is to learn how to relax our bodies."

Now the facilitator teaches the children a few breathing exercises:
Teens are asked to take in a big breath and let it out. "Now take in another big breath, hold it and count to 10. 1–2–3–4–5–6–7–8–9–10. Then let it go." Now the teens take in a normal breath and sigh with a slight sound. Have the teens do it again.

DRAWING SHEET

ME Before the Death   ME After the Death

DRAWING SHEET

MY BEST MEMORY

DRAWING SHEET

My Last Memory

DRAWING SHEET

Something that makes me (or has made me)
Since the Death of My Special Person

MAD

SAD

SCARED

HAPPY

DRAWING SHEET

This is what death looks like to me

DRAWING SHEET

This is what I remember about the day my special person died.

DRAWING SHEET

This is what I remember about the funeral

FEELING CIRCLE

FEELING FACES SHEET

MORE FEELINGS

FEELINGS OF GRIEF LIST

Add more if you like
(to be used with Journal Sheet #4)

Happy	Frustrated	Peaceful
Guilty	Secure	Bitter
Angry	Worried	Irritated
Sad	Confused	Relieved
Carefree	Excited	Lonely
Tense	Hopeless	Paralyzed
Drained	Hurt	Confident
Afraid	Overwhelmed	Invisible

FEELINGS SENTENCE STARTERS

I get frustrated when . . .	When I am mad I . . .
I feel close to . . .	I want to eat when I feel . . .
I feel lonely when . . .	I am not close to . . .
One feeling that is easy for my family to express is . . .	When I am happy I . . .
I feel mad when . . .	I am confused about . . .
I show my feelings to . . .	I never feel . . .

FEELINGS SENTENCE STARTERS

I always feel . . .	I hide my feelings from . . .
When I am sad I . . .	I feel overwhelmed when . . .
It's hard to fall asleep when . . .	I get excited when . . .
One feeling that is hard for my family to express . . .	When I worry I . . .
I feel good about myself when . . .	I worry about . . .

FEELINGS SENTENCE STARTERS

I feel different from other
kids when . . .

I feel misunderstood by . . .

It is not hard to share
my feelings with . . .

It's hard to share my
feelings with . . .

I feel happy when . . .

FIGHT CARDS

Feeling angry about the loss.	Being afraid that I'm losing control because my feelings are so intense.
Taking care of other people keeps me from thinking about the death.	Feeling scared to share what I've been thinking, feeling, and doing.
Thinking that if I try hard enough I can bring back what I lost.	Wanting someone punished for the loss.
Not believing that this loss happened.	Needing to tell others what happened.

FIGHT CARDS

Going over the loss in my mind, trying to figure out how it could have been different.

Keeping active to avoid thinking about what happened.

Avoiding being alone.

Thinking I am responsible for the loss.

Feeling like I am going crazy.

Trying to hold back my tears.

Trying to figure out why this happened to me.

Being afraid to think about anything else except the loss of my special person.

FIGHT CARDS

Keeping reminders of my loved one around me.	Hoping that I am dreaming and will wake up and find out it never happened.

FLIGHT CARDS

Wondering what point
there is in going on.

Putting away anything that
reminds me of the loss of
my special person.

Thinking I am better off
without my special person.

Feeling detached and
separate from others.

Being careless.

Feeling irritated with other
people.

Trying not to let anything
affect me.

Avoiding telling anyone
what I'm thinking, feeling,
and/or doing.

FLIGHT CARDS

Feeling confused and disoriented.	Thinking that even if I could understand why my special person died, it wouldn't change anything
Avoid feeling too sad about the loss of my special person.	Feeling bored with life.
Feeling overwhelmed.	Thinking it's best not to dwell on the past.
Refusing to talk about the loss of my special person.	Avoiding people who remind me of my special person.

FLIGHT CARDS

Believing something else is going to go wrong.

Acting as though this doesn't matter to me.

The things I used to enjoy aren't fun anymore.

FUNERAL PHOTOS

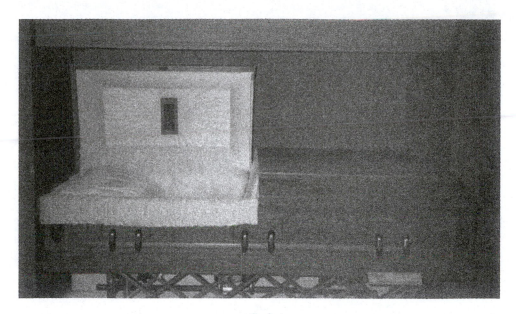

Casket

Casket

FUNERAL PHOTOS

Urn

Urn

FUNERAL PHOTOS

Altar

Cemetery

FUNERAL PHOTOS

Cemetery

Hospital

FUNERAL PHOTOS

Church

Funeral Home

Grief Keys

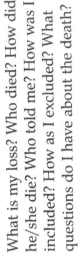

GETTING THE FACTS

What is my loss? Who died? How did he/she die? Who told me? How was I included? How as I excluded? What questions do I have about the death?

1. Find someone who can answer your questions.
2. Find someone you can talk to about your loss. Tell your story over and over again.

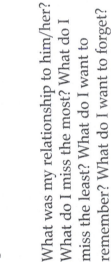

REMEMBERING

What was my relationship to him/her? What do I miss the most? What do I miss the least? What do I want to remember? What do I want to forget?

1. Look at pictures, films, and video tapes. Talk about it. Do it over and over again.
2. Recall the special person with stories and memories.
3. Remember your special person on important days.

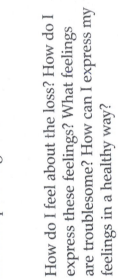

IDENTIFYING CHANGES

What changes have I experienced since the death? How have I changed? How has my family changed? How have my friendships changed? How has school changed?

1. Return to a routine as soon as possible.
2. Keep the changes to a minimum.
3. Identify and talk about changes.

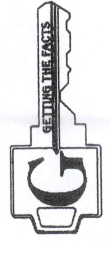

EXPRESSING FEELINGS

How do I feel about the loss? How do I express these feelings? What feelings are troublesome? How can I express my feelings in a healthy way?

1. Express your feelings by talking, writing, drawing, listening to music, and through physical exercise.
2. Tell someone you trust how you feel.

FINDING HELP

Who does/does not give me help? What kind of help do I need? Where can I get help?

1. Identify different people who can give you different kinds of support.
2. Ask for help from those you trust.
3. Seek out others who have had a similar loss.

GRIEF SUPPORT GROUPS GENERAL INFORMATION SHEET (GIS)

Child's name: _____

Today's date: _____ Date that the loss occurred: _____

First time participant in group? Yes _____ No _____

If no, how many times has your child participated in a group

prior to the current group? _____

Who died?

Mother _____ Father _____ Sibling _____ Friend _____

Relative (specify) _____ Other (specify) _____

How close was the child to the person that died?

Not at all close _____ Somewhat close _____ Close _____ Pretty close _____

Very close _____

What was the cause of the death?

Illness _____ Accident _____ Sudden death (e.g., heart attack) _____

Suicide _____ Homicide _____

Did the child witness the death?

Yes _____ No _____

With whom does the child currently live?

Parent _____ (specify) Mother _____ Father _____ Sibling _____

Friend _____ Relative (specify) _____ Other (specify) _____

Who provides the child's primary emotional support? (All that apply)

Parent _____ Sibling _____ Friend _____ Relative (specify) _____

Mental health practitioner (specify) _____

Religious representative (e.g., nun, pastor, rabbi, priest) _____

Other (specify) _____

What other losses has the child experienced in his or her lifetime? (All that apply)

Death of a parent (specify) _____ Date of loss _____

Death of sibling (specify age of sibling) _____ Date of loss _____

Death of friend (specify) _____ Date of loss _____

Death of relative (specify) _____ Date of loss _____

Death of other significant person (specify) _____ Date of loss _____

Loss of home (specify) _____ Date of loss _____

Separation from sibling(s) (specify) _____ Date of loss _____

Loss of biological family unit: Foster care _____ or Adoption _____

Date of loss _____

Had the child experienced any of the following prior to the loss? (All that apply)

Physical abuse _____ When _____Relationship to perpetrator _____

Sexual abuse _____ When _____ Relationship to perpetrator _____

Depression _____ When _____

Suicide attempt (s) _____ When _____

Addiction/substance abuse _____ When _____

School

Does your child receive any special assistance at school such as tutoring, advanced placement, or special classes? (specify)

_____

_____

_____

Has the school environment been supportive of your child or have there been problems since the death? (provide details)

_____

_____

_____

Reaction to Loss

How does your child most easily express him- or herself (talking, writing, art, physical games)?

_____

_____

_____

What would you like the group facilitator to know about your child?

_____

_____

_____

Relationships

How would you describe your relationship with your child? How does your child relate to other family members?

_____

_____

_____

How would you describe your child's relationship with peers (ages of peers, extrovert, introvert, leader, follower)?

_____

_____

_____

Health

Does your child have any health concerns? Any allergies? Has he or she had any serious injuries or illnesses? Is your child taking any medications?

_____

What is your child's most frequent health problem?

_____

Will you give permission for a group picture to be taken?

Yes _____ No _____

GRIEF REACTION CARDS—EMOTIONAL

Irritability	Mood swings
Marked changes in behavior (either for the better or worse)	Panic (an overwhelming fear of danger to self or others)
Hyper or hypoactivity	Detachment

GRIEF REACTION CARDS—MENTAL

Shorter attention span	Short term memory loss
Difficulty concentrating	Distractedness
Preoccupation with the loss	

GRIEF REACTION CARDS—PHYSICAL

Overactive or underactive	Tingling in the arms
Fast heartbeat	Diarrhea
No energy	Tired a lot
Hard to eat	Stomachaches

GRIEF REACTION CARDS—PHYSICAL

Hungrier	Get sick a lot
Eating problems	

GRIEF REACTION CARDS—SOCIAL

Spend a lot of time alone	School work is harder
Have a hard time sitting still	Get into trouble more
Don't get into trouble at all anymore	Fight with people more
Sometimes you act younger than you are	A drop in school grades

GRIEF REACTION CARDS—SOCIAL

Act or try to be like the special person that died	Don't want to leave home
Break things	Can't talk about the loss
Steal things from others	Do things that are at high risk and could hurt you
Miss school a lot	Takes care of other people too much

GRIEF REACTION CARDS—SOCIAL

Act older than most kids my age	Don't get along with friends or other family members

GRIEF REACTION CARDS—WARNING SIGNS

Destructive behavior	Compulsive caregiving, taking on too much responsibility
Independence beyond one's years	Stealing
Depression	Substance abuse
Early sexual activity or promiscuity	Stuck at an early developmental stage

GRIEF REACTION CARDS—WARNING SIGNS

Difficulty in relationships	School Phobia
Increased fighting and aggression	Eating disorders
Risk-taking	Cannot talk about the loss of my special person
Over-identification with the loss of my special person	A drop in school performance that is sustained

GROUP EVALUATION FORM

Date: _____ Group:_____

Facilitators: _____

I would rate this group:

1	2	3	4	5
Poor		OK		Great

This is what I liked about the group:

One thing I would change is:

One thing I would like to say to the facilitators is:

I felt the facilitators care about me:

1	2	3	4	5
Strongly Disagree		Agree		Strongly Agree

Other Comments:

Journal Sheet #1

(to be used with the Adjective List)

Three words that would describe me are:

_____

_____

_____

These words are represented by the colors:

_____

_____

_____

A word that might describe me since the death of my special person might be:

_____

That word is represented by the color:

_____

If I were to give myself a "new name" since the death of my special person, it would be:

_____

My "new name" means:

_____

Journal Sheet #2

List your family members/friends and choose a bead color that represents each person:

_____

_____

_____

Now, think of three words that describe each person:

_____

_____

_____

What word and color bead would describe each person in your family/friend since the death of your special person?

_____

_____

_____

_____

_____

_____

What word best describes your family/friends as a whole?

_____

That word is represented by the color:

_____

Journal Sheet #3

When I think of my special person who died, three words come to mind:

_____

_____

_____

These words are represented by the colors:

_____

_____

_____

One word that describes our relationship is:

_____

That word is represented by the color:

_____

One thing I never want to forget about him/her is:

_____

_____

_____

That is represented by the color:

_____

Journal Sheet #4

(to be used with the Feelings of Grief List)

Since my special person died, I am feeling these feelings:

_____

_____

These feelings are represented by the colors:

_____

_____

I wish I could feel:

_____

_____

_____

That feeling is represented by the color:

_____

One feeling that is troublesome is:

_____

That feeling is represented by the color:

_____

I can share my feeling with:

_____

That person is represented by the color:

_____

Journal Sheet #5

Three healthy ways that I deal with my feelings are: (please pick a bead color for each):

_____

_____

_____

Three words I think describe our group are: (please pick a bead color for each):

_____

_____

_____

A good name for our group is:

_____

That name means:

_____

_____

_____

It is represented by the color:

_____

❤ *L O V E   N O T E S* ❤

MEMORY CARDS

Remember a gift your special person gave to you	Remember something you gave your special person
Remember a sad memory with your special person	Remember a birthday from your past with your special person
Remember a happy memory with your special person	Remember a way your special person helped you out
Remember a holiday in the past with your special person	Remember a neighborhood memory with your special person

MEMORY CARDS

Remember an angry memory
with your special person

Remember an outside memory
with your special person

Remember a scary memory
with your special person

Remember a winter memory
with your special person

Remember a trip you took
with your special person

Remember a meal with
your special person

Remember a special event
with your special person

Remember something you
did together for fun

MEMORY CARDS

Remember a big family gathering with your special person	Remember a summer memory with your special person
Remember something funny that happened with your special person	Remember something you did at night with your special person*

*Note: this card should not be used if a child has been sexually abused by the caregiver who died.

PRESCRIPTIONS FOR FEELINGS

Prescription

For: *Scared*

1.   Tell someone, "I am scared because . . ."
2.   Get a hug.
3.   Listen to soft music.
4.   Breathe deeply.
5.   Tell yourself, "I will be okay."
6.   Exercise.
7.   Take a warm bath.

Prescription

For: *Sad*

1.   Tell someone, "I am sad because . . ."
2.   Cry.
3.   Get a hug.
4.   Write about it.
5.   Draw your sadness.
6.   Exercise.
7.   Watch a funny show.

Prescription

For: *Mad*

1.   Run around the block.
2.   Tell someone, "I am mad because . . ."
3.   Go outside and scream.
4.   Punch your pillow.
5.   Draw your anger.
6.   Rip up old newspapers (be sure to clean up).
7.   Count to 10 slowly. Breathe deeply.

PROBLEM-SOLVING PLAN HANDOUT

1. Stop!! What is the problem?

2. What are some plans?

3. What is the best plan?

4. Do the plan.

5. Did the plan work?

PROBLEM-SOLVING SCENARIOS

1. Other kids make fun of me.

2. I am scared to talk to others about my feelings.

3. I can't concentrate on my schoolwork.

4. Nobody wants to hang out with me.

5. I don't know what to say when people ask me about the death.

6. Sometimes I'm so depressed I don't want to do anything.

7. I'm using drugs and alcohol so I don't have to think about my feelings.

PUZZLE PIECES

RELAXATION ACTIVITY

GENERAL INSTRUCTIONS

Always begin an imagery by preparing the group for it. Invite teens to participate in the imagery. Tell them what you are going to do. Teens should not be forced to partici-pate, it should be voluntary. If a teen chooses not to participate, encourage them to be respectful of others who would like to participate. Instruct the teens to lay comfortably on the floor, arms resting comfortably at their sides. If there is any clothing that feels tight, they should loosen it. Begin by having teens close their eyes. ALWAYS BEGIN AN IMAGERY BY DOING SOME GENERAL BODY RELAXATION. This relaxation should include tensing muscles and releasing, starting from the toes, and moving up to the top of the head. As different parts of the body begin to relax, facilitator sets the stage by explaining that for the next several minutes each person will totally focus on themselves. There may be distracting noises out in the hall or in the parking lot. Try not to pay too much attention to these sounds, just let them be there. Focus on your breath-ing, your body feels relaxed. After the group appears to be relaxed and ready to begin the imagery you may begin. . . .

"We are going to take an imaginary trip. Imagine that we leave this room and go down the hall to the door. Outside of the door waiting for you is a hot air balloon. The balloon has beautiful bright colors on it and across the middle of it is written your name. This is your very own balloon. You climb inside the balloon and it takes off. You have control over how high off the ground the balloon will go. The basket that you stand in has high sides so that you don't have to worry about falling out. You feel very safe. As the balloon takes off, you feel excited about the trip you are about to take. The balloon begins to float through the air. You float over trees and lakes, streets and high-ways. You see cars below and planes above you. You see shopping malls, schools, and office buildings. Eventually, you only see countryside—trees, fields, lakes, and streams. As the balloon moves along it doesn't make any sound. Soon you see off in the dis-tance, the deep, blue ocean and a sandy beach. You can hear the roar of the water. You notice that the air is getting warmer. The closer you get to the beach you can see the clear, white sand. The balloon begins to descend as you reach your destination. The balloon lands softly on the sand. You get off of the balloon and start walking down the beach so that you can find a spot to lay in the sun. After you find your spot, you lay down in the warm sand. You feel very relaxed and happy to be there. The sky is clear and the sun is warm. You can feel the sun on your body. The sun makes you feel very relaxed. You hear the waves splash against the shore. The waves go in and out, in and out. They seem to match your breathing. You breathe in and out, in and out. With every breath you take in, you feel relaxed. With every breath you let out, you let go of tension. You hear the seagulls calling above you and the voices of others in the far sand and the sand trickles through your fingers. You feel very relaxed. Lay here for a while and enjoy how relaxed you feel. Remember how this moment feels." LONG PAUSE.................

Now we will come back to the group. Remember, you can return to this beach whenever you choose. Whenever you are ready, open your eyes.

RESOURCE LIST

PHONE NUMBERS TO CALL IF YOU NEED HELP BETWEEN GROUPS

FIRST CALL FOR HELP _____

CRISIS CONNECTION _____

CHILDREN'S MENTAL HEALTH CRISIS LINE _____

TEEN LINE_____

CRISIS INTERVENTION _____

SUICIDE HOTLINE _____

CENTER FOR GRIEF, LOSS, & TRANSITION_____

STORY CARDS

Did you know that your special person was going to die?	How were you told that your special person was going to die?
If it was unexpected, how did you find out about the death?	Who told you about the death and what did they tell you?
What do you think happened?	Were you with your special person when he or she died? Tell us about that.
What time of day did your special person die?	How did you feel when you found out that your special person died?

STORY CARDS

How did your body feel when you found out your special person died?	Who helped you on the days around the funeral?
Did you go to the visitation? If so, what do you remember about it?	Did you go to the funeral?
Did you get to see the body? If you did, what was it like seeing the body? If you did not get to see the body, what was that like?	Did you get to say goodbye to your special person who died?
Did you participate in the funeral?	What do you remember about the funeral?

STORY CARDS

What do you remember about the cemetery?

Are there any questions you have about the death that no one has answered for you?

Where do you think your special person is now?

What do you remember about the last time you saw your special person alive?

Did you have a feeling that your special person was going to die?

After your special person died, what is something that someone said to you that you thought was stupid?

After your special person died, what is something that someone said to you that you thought was helpful?

What reminds you of your special person?

STORY CARDS

What do you see that makes you think about him/her?	Did you make your special person die?
Can you wish someone dead and then they will die?	Can you still talk to your special person?
Do you ever talk to your special person?	Do you think that your special person hears you?
Does your special person watch over you?	Did you get to see the body of your special person who died?

STORY CARDS

Was the body buried in the ground or was it cremated? What do you remember about that?	What do you remember about when your special person died?

SUPPORT WHEEL

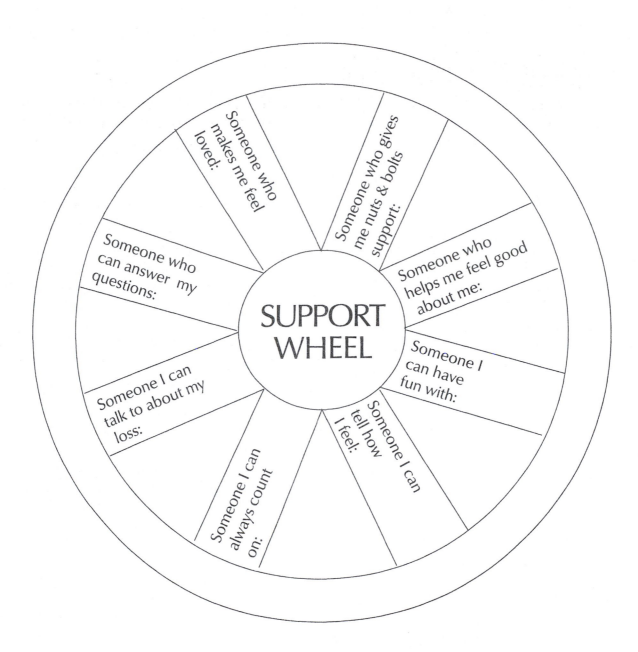

THOUGHT-STOPPING WORKSHEET

Thought-stopping is a technique we can use whenever our thoughts make us feel bad about ourselves or our situation. Here is an example of a way to use thought-stopping:

ME PUT-DOWNS
"No one likes me because I'm so dumb and ugly. I don't have any friends. I am nothing!"

Now say to yourself....................   **"STOP!"**

REPLACE YOUR THOUGHT WITH A NEW THOUGHT: "I am not dumb and ugly. It may feel like no one likes me but I know someone cares about me. I am important."

Now try it with these examples:

SAD
"I am so unhappy since my special person died. I don't care about anything. I will never be happy again!"

STOP!

NEW THOUGHT:

MAD
"I hate _____. He/she makes me so mad! I don't want him/her for a friend anymore. I don't care if I ever see or talk to him/her again!"

STOP!

NEW THOUGHT:

WORRIED
"What will happen if my caregiver dies? Who will take care of me? Where will I live? What if I die?"

STOP!

NEW THOUGHT:

WHAT I THINK ABOUT DEATH CARDS

Death is contagious.	Most people don't want to talk about death.
When a special person dies, most families/friends pull together.	When a special person dies, they know what you're thinking and doing at all times.
Sometimes I think my special person could have prevented his/her death.	All things happen of a reason, even bad things.
When things go wrong, sometimes I feel like I'm being punished.	When someone dies, someone is born to replace them.
I will "see" my special person who died again some day.	Sometimes I think I could have prevented the death of my special person.

WHAT I THINK ABOUT DEATH CARDS

Sometimes I "feel" the dead person is with me. I feel his/her presence.

I can recover from this and be healthy and happy.

Sometimes I talk to the person who died.

I worry that I might die in the same way.

Bad things happen to good people.

When someone dies, they watch over you and protect you.

When a special person dies, it's important to carry on certain parts of their personality, or the role he/she played in the family.

Sample Notes to be Sent Home to Caregivers

Week 2: Telling My Story

We started our group today with a song, "Lean on Me," which is how we will begin each session. After that, we got to know each other by writing some things about ourselves on a puzzle piece and sharing them. Then we all put the puzzle together. We then developed a Code of Safety so that we can all feel comfortable expressing ourselves in the group. We got a resource list with some numbers we can call for help. Tonight we learned what a check-in is. A check-in is a time each week when we share with each other how we are feeling. Next we talked about what grief means and talked about the first grief key: Getting the Facts. Then we played a game where we each told each other some things about who died, how they died, etc. After that we drew either what we remember about the death of our special person or the funeral. Then we lit a candle and we each got an affirmation.

Week 3: Exploring Death

We started our group with our song again and then we had a centering activity. A centering activity is a time that we spend quieting down from the day and getting ourselves ready for group. Then we had a check-in. Then we talked about what 'dead' means and continued to talk about the first grief key: Getting the Facts. We discussed concepts such as "all living things die," "death is irreversible," and "death is not contagious." Next we played a game that explores what we personally think about death. Then we looked at some funeral photos and talked about these things (i.e., casket, cemetery, urn, etc.). The most important thing we learned today is that we need to keep asking questions to someone we can trust so we can get our questions answered. We wrote in our journals, as we will do almost every week, and began picking beads for a beaded wristband we are making, which will tell our stories. We ended the group by picking our weekly affirmation.

Week 4: Identifying Changes

We began our group with our song again and then had a centering activity. After that we had a check-in. Then we talked about change and the third grief key: Identifying Changes. We talked about how when a special person dies, there can be lots of changes. These are changes we did not create. We discussed the changes around us everyday. We played a game where we each picked a card and said whether or not we have experienced the changes written on the cards since the death of our special person. We learned that we have had lots of changes since our special person died. Next we drew a picture of ourselves before and after the death. Then we played another game, where we explored how we reacted/are reacting to the changes in our lives since the death of our special person. We talked about common grief reactions and how they change over time. We wrote in our journals and then ended the group by picking our weekly affirmation.

Caregiver: Next week your teen should bring a picture of his or her special person to group as well as something that reminds him or her of that person.

Week 5: Memories/Remembering

We began our group with our song again and then had a centering activity. Then we had a check-in. After that we talked about the second grief key: Remembering. We learned that it's important to talk about memories and remember our special person who died so that we don't forget them. Then we spent some time sharing the pictures and belongings of our special person that we brought to group. We played a memory game. We wrote in our journals. Then we did a candle ceremony which reminds us that even though our special person is no longer with us, we will always remember that they were here with us and still are here in our memories. We ended the group by picking our weekly affirmation.

Caregiver: Tonight your teen is bringing home a candle to burn in memory of his or her special person. We urge you to caution your child to burn the candle only in the presence of an adult.

Week 6: Identifying and Expressing Feelings

We began our group with our song again. Then we had a centering activity. Then we had a check-in. Then we talked about the fourth grief key: Expressing Feelings. We talked about feelings. We learned that when a special person dies, it's okay to have lots of different feelings. We then did an activity where we used feeling words to complete sentences. Then we played a game where we picked cards and determined whether we are coping with the death of our special person with "fight" (where we don't let ourselves feel our feelings) or "flight" (where we ignore our feelings) reactions. Then we wrote in our weekly journals. We ended the group by picking our weekly affirmation.

Week 7: Exploring Unfinished Business

We started our group with our song again and then did a centering activity. Then we had a check-in. Then we talked about our topic: Unfinished Business. We learned that sometimes when a special person dies, we don't get to say good-bye to him or her. Sometimes there are things we didn't get to do with that person, and there are things we don't get to do with them anymore. Those are the things we talked about tonight. We played a game called "coulda-woulda-shoulda" to explore things that we think we could, should, or would have done differently with our special person. Then we talked about and symbolically let go of some of these. Then we drew a picture of the last memory we have of our special person. Next, we each wrote a love note to our special person. We learned that even though our special person has died, we can still talk to him or her and remember him or her. We ended the group by picking our weekly affirmation.

Caregiver: The teens spent some time writing a love note to their special people tonight. We encourage you to spend some time with your teen talking to him or her about what he or she would like to do with the note. Does your teen want to take it to the cemetery? Keep it in a special place? Burn it? (in your presence, of course). These love notes are intended to encourage the teens to communicate with their special people. Talking with your teen about the love note affords you the opportunity to talk with your teen about the death of the special person.

Also, please call the group facilitator if you wish to schedule a conference to discuss your teen's bereavement. You may schedule to meet either before or after next week's session (week 8) or the following week (week 9).

Week 8: Coping with Feelings

We began our group with our song again. Then we had a centering activity. After that we had a check-in. Then we continued to talk about the fourth grief key: Expressing Feelings, specifically coping with those feelings. We talked about what can happen to our feelings if we don't get them out. We used a balloon to show what can happen. If we keep blowing air into the balloon, eventually it will pop and break. That's what can happen to us if we don't get our feelings out. They will get bigger and bigger until we can't hold them in anymore and our feelings will pop out. We talked about things that might indicate that we are not coping with our feelings (i.e., getting in fights at school, drugs, withdrawing, etc.). We learned how to cope with our feelings in a healthy way; one technique is thought stopping. We learned that when we have a thought that makes us feel bad, we can replace it with another thought. Then we took a break and played with bubble wrap. Then we drew or sculpted "sad." Then we looked at some prescriptions for feelings and learned some ways to help us with our feelings: some healthy ways to let them out. Then we threw wet sponges at a mad target to help us express our anger. Then we wrote in our weekly journal and ended the group by picking our weekly affirmation.

Caregiver: Next week there will be a group picture taken. Your teen will get a copy of the picture to take home with him or her on the last night of group.

Also, please call the group facilitator if you wish to schedule a conference to discuss your teen's bereavement. You may schedule to meet either before or after next week's session (week 9).

Week 9: Learning About Self-Care And Support

We began our group with our song again and had a centering activity. Then we had our check-in. Then we talked about self-care and support which is part of the fifth grief key: Finding Help. We found out that self-care means taking care of ourselves. We also talked about support. We learned that support means "help." Then we filled in a support wheel to identify who can give us different kinds of support. Then we learned to use a problem solving plan that can help us solve problems. Next we did some relaxation exercises and monitored our bodies with Bio-dots®. Then we beaded a wristband; the colors of the beads are symbolic, as we have been picking them out each week as we wrote in our journal. We shared the meaning of our wristbands with each other. Then we ended the group by picking our weekly affirmation.

Caregiver: Next week is the last night of group. Refreshments will be served after the session and you are invited to attend this portion of the session.

Week 10: Learning To Say Good-Bye

We started our group with our song and then had a centering activity. After that we had a check-in. We talked about saying good-bye and did our group evaluations. Next we each wrote an affirmation, or something that we appreciated about each person in the group. We brought these home. Instead of writing in our journal, we wrote a letter to future group members. Next we ended the group by taking out the puzzle pieces that we designed during the first week. We then talked about how we are all connected and what we have learned over the past 10 weeks. We took our puzzle pieces home to remind us that we are all connected to each other. We had some snacks and then said 'good-bye' to the other group members.

Special Activities: Holidays

Valentine's Day: An activity that can be fun for teens on Valentine's Day is to bring heart-shaped cookies and a tub of frosting and let the teens decorate their own cookies.

Mother's Day and Father's Day: If a teen has had a parent die, both holidays are difficult. The parent who died may have helped in planning the celebrations and in buying or making gifts. For example, if the mother died, the teen may not have the resources to make a Father's Day gift. The day serves a heightened reminder of the loss. In other words, teens are acutely aware of the loss of their father on Father's Day. In group, it is important to talk about the holiday during check-in and ask people what they are feeling about it. It may also be appropriate to make a gift during group. It can help to talk about how even though the parent died, he or she is still the teen's parent and the teen might want to remember their parent with a gift that can be left at the grave or kept someplace special.

Independence Day: Fireworks are often the most exciting part of the Fourth of July for kids. Use fireworks to talk about the feelings they have. Ask them how fireworks are like feelings. Fireworks change color; some are loud and scary; some make us happy; some fireworks last a long time; sometimes they are duds. Have them color a picture of what sets off their feeling fireworks.

Thanksgiving: Because families gather together at this time, many feelings may resurface for the teens because of the absence of their special person. These aspects of the holiday should be discussed in group. The group may also discuss "giving thanks" for living family members or for the special memories they have of their special person.

Christmas/Hanukkah/Kwanzaa: These holidays may evoke the same feelings as does Thanksgiving. It can be helpful to talk with teens about special holiday traditions they shared with their special person. How can they remember their special person during this time? Maybe they want to continue a tradition that they used to share with their special person or maybe they want to do something different. Help the teens find ways to talk with their family about what they are feeling and what would be helpful to them during the holidays.

Birthdays: Celebrating birthdays in a time-limited group is hard because not everyone's birthday falls during the session. Those teens whose birthdays are at other times of the year may feel left out. Birthdays can be acknowledged during check-in and it can be an opportunity to talk about how birthdays feel when our loved ones have died. If the teens really want to celebrate, have an Unbirthday Party for everyone in the group. Wrap little gift boxes with questions in them that pertain to the gifts received from the person who died. Questions could include: what is something special my special person gave me?; what is a quality that I share with my special person?; what did my special person teach me that I always want to remember?

Sample Curriculum for a Special Day

▧ Holiday Heartaches

This session is intended for use when a holiday falls during the week of the group meeting. These holiday themes can be incorporated into the grief curriculum to help the teens through the holidays, which can be especially difficult times. Activities during this session may be incorporated into any of the sessions. The teens can share feelings surrounding their holiday experience. They can also make gifts for their special people, for example, Christmas/Hanukkah/Kwanzaa presents to help remember their special people and to share the holiday with them. The holiday session is important given that during these times, issues surrounding the loss are especially salient.

Objectives

To remember the teen's special person from holidays past
To remember holidays from the past
To identify how holidays are different now
To talk about ways to remember the teen's special person during the holidays

Materials

Centering activity overview
Centering candle
Crayons
Feeling face sheet
Gift bag
Gift boxes
Christmas, Kwanzaa, Hanukkah items
Matches

Memory sheet
Sun-catcher or remembrance (tree) ornament
Gold elastic string
Large translucent beads (red, white, clear)
Pipe cleaners
Ribbon to match

Procedures

Note: A star (*) by an activity denotes that this is a main activity, considered central to the session. Unstarred activities are supplemental activities.

Opening Activity*

Use the same procedures outlined in Week 2.

Centering Activity*

Materials
    Centering activity overview
    Centering candle
    Matches
    (See Appendix 2)

Use the same procedures outlined in Week 3.

Sharing Feelings (Check-In)*

Materials
    Crayons
    Feeling face sheets
    (See Appendix 2 for sample feeling face sheets)

Teens check-in by circling a face on the feeling faces sheet. Facilitator asks the following questions: "What are you dreading about the holidays? What are you looking forward to? What will you do the same? What will you do different? Is it okay to be happy and excited about the holidays? How will you remember their special person over the holidays? Is there some way you can memorialize them?"

Introduction To The Topic: Holiday Heartaches*

Materials
    Christmas, Kwanzaa, Hanukkah Items

"Tonight we are going to talk about the holidays that we will be celebrating in a short while. What holidays are coming up? (Christmas? Kwanzaa? Hanukah?) When a special person dies, we really miss them around the holiday season and our holiday may be different from other years. We remember your special person who died, and we remember holidays that we spent with them in the past. Let's see if we can recall certain memories about the upcoming holidays." Give each one of the teens an item from the holiday. Have some symbols from Christmas, Kwanzaa, and Hanukkah.

Examples of things to bring are:

Angels	Kwanzaa candles
Bells	Menorah
Candy canes	Reindeer
Christmas lights	Santa
Christmas tree decorations	Snowmen
Christmas wreath	Tree
Dreidel	Wrapping paper

Pass out one of these things to each of the teens. Teens then take turns talking about the item that they have and if they have any memories of this item. Remind the teens that these things remind people of the holidays and when the holidays are celebrated this year they will also remind us of his or her special person who died because that person is no longer with the teen to celebrate the holidays. Teens are encouraged to recall any memories they have of that item with their special person.

Gifts From Our Special People

Materials
Gift bag
Gift boxes
Memory sheet
(See last page of this Appendix for memory sheet)

Explain that "When we celebrate holidays this time of year, we often give gifts to each other. Tonight we are going to open up our very special gifts to share with each other. These gifts are not toys or things we can play with, but rather are gifts our special person gave us in the form of a memory. We will each take turns picking a gift from the pouch. Inside of the gift box you will find a very special memory that your special person who died has given to you in the form of a memory. Remember what a memory is?" Each teen then opens his or her gift and talks about what memory they have that is printed on the slip of paper inside. Explain that even though the teen's special person cannot be with him or her this year, they have given the teen a very special gift in the form of a memory that can always be kept.

Remembrance (Tree) Ornament or Sun-Catcher

Materials
Gold elastic string
Large translucent beads (red, white, clear)
Pipecleaners
Ribbon to match

Explain, "Now we are going to remember your special person who died by making something in memory of your special person. You can choose to make a tree ornament or a sun-catcher to hang in your window at home. Decide what shape you want your ornament or sun-catcher to be. Suggestions are a heart or star. Now thread your beads through the pipe cleaner until you have enough to shape it."

Closing*

Use the same procedures outlined in Week 2.

MEMORY SHEET

Remember a gift he/she gave you

Remember a gift you gave him/her

Remember your holiday last year

Remember a holiday when your special person was alive

If your special person was here with you this year, what gift would she/he give you?

Something you did with your special person around the holidays

A TV show that you watched together around the holidays

A holiday movie that you watched with your special person

Remember something you did on New Year's Eve

Remember decorating the tree with your special person

Remember something funny around the holiday

Remember a holiday meal you ate with your special person

Index

About the Authors

Linda Lehmann, M.A., is the founder and former Executive Director of the Center for Grief, Loss, and Transition in St. Paul, Minnesota. She has worked with children and adolescents for more than 30 years and has worked within the grief and loss arena since 1987. Linda Lehmann is a licensed psychologist in private practice in St. Paul and is the Bereavement Coordinator for the Children's Hospitals and Clinics in the Twin Cities.

Shane R. Jimerson, Ph.D., is a professor of Developmental Studies and Counseling, Clinical, and School Psychology in the Graduate School of Education at the University of California in Santa Barbara (UCSB). Dr. Jimerson is also the Director of Project Loss at UCSB, where he studies grief and the transitions that children and families experience following a loss.

Ann Gaasch, M.A., has worked with children and families since 1991, specializing in issues of bereavement, trauma, and abuse. She is a family therapist with the Harriet Tubman Family Center in Minnesota and is associated with the Center for Grief, Loss, and Transition in St. Paul, Minnesota.

CPSIA information can be obtained
at www.ICGtesting.com
Printed in the USA
BVOW07s0844010617

485767BV00011B/118/P